COUNSELLING IN FURTHER
AND HIGHER EDUCATION

· COUNSELLING IN CONTEXT ·

Series editors
Moira Walker and Michael Jacobs
University of Leicester

Counselling takes place in many different contexts: in voluntary and statutory agencies; in individual private practice or in a consortium; at work, in medical settings, in churches and in different areas of education. While there may be much in common in basic counselling methods (despite theoretical differences), each setting gives rise to particular areas of concern, and often requires specialist knowledge, both of the problems likely to be brought, but also of the context in which the client is being seen. Even common counselling issues vary slightly from situation to situation in the way they are applied and understood.

This series examines eleven such areas, and applies a similar scheme to each, first looking at the history of the development of counselling in that particular context; then at the context itself, and how the counsellor fits into it. Central to each volume are chapters on common issues related to the specific setting and questions that may be peculiar to it but could be of interest and value to counsellors working elsewhere. Each book will provide useful information for anyone considering counselling, or the provision of counselling in a particular context. Relationships with others who work in the same setting whether as counsellors, managers or administrators are also examined; and each book concludes with the author's own critique of counselling as it is currently practised in that context.

Current and forthcoming titles

COUNSELLING IN FURTHER AND HIGHER EDUCATION

Elsa Bell

OPEN UNIVERSITY PRESS
Buckingham · Philadelphia

Open University Press
Celtic Court
22 Ballmoor
Buckingham
MK18 1XW

and

1900 Frost Road, Suite 101
Bristol, PA 19007, USA

First Published 1996

A catalogue record of this book is available from the British Library

ISBN 0 335 19167 3 (pb)

Library of Congress Cataloging-in-Publication Data
Bell, Elsa, 1947–
Counselling in further and higher education / Elsa Bell.
p. cm. — (Counselling in context)
Includes bibliographical references and index.
ISBN 0–335–19167–3 (pbk.)
1. Counselling in higher education—Great Britain. I. Title.
II. Series.
LB2343.B397   1996
378.1'94—dc20   96–481   CIP

Typeset by Graphicraft Typesetting Ltd, Hong Kong
Printed in Great Britain by St Edmundsbury Press Ltd,
Bury St Edmunds, Suffolk

Contents

Series editors' preface

This particular context for counselling, Higher and Further Education, is the area of work in which both editors have learned their craft. This has meant that Elsa Bell's book is of particular significance to us. We can remember the time when counselling as a whole was largely represented by Marriage Guidance counsellors (as it was then known), by student counsellors, and by pastoral counsellors. We have ourselves worked virtually alone in counselling services at a time when university populations were smaller and when many academics wondered why a counselling service should be at all necessary. We have seen counselling in universities and colleges of higher and further education assume its real importance, providing immediate and invaluable assistance to young people as many of them, for the first time in their lives, hit their first real crises. We have been responsible for the development of services, for the increase in the number of staff, and the use of placement and sessional staff in order to meet demand. We have recognized that, these young people are especially fortunate to have such help available to them in a world that often denies similar help to others of their age, and we have worked for similar access to counselling for the wider population. We have been glad to see counselling services extended in colleges of further education.

There is much here for which to be grateful, and Elsa Bell has documented the way these developments have taken place, including a generous tribute to our own immediate predecessor, perhaps the very first student counsellor in this country, Mary Swainson. We have noted, however, other changes that constantly remind us that there is no way in which student counsellors can be complacent: we have recognized how many young people (or indeed mature students) have sought help with long standing and deeply disturbing circumstances. It has not been university or college life that has provoked their first real crisis, but it has been university or college life which has provided the first haven from crisis in the family, and therefore the first real opportunity for help. We have noted with concern the way in which universities and colleges, in their need for student numbers, can sometimes select students who are not able to cope with the pressures of modern tertiary education, where the institutions are so large that it can be difficult to get specific academic help. We have felt angry at the way in which just a few academic institutions have treated their counselling services in search of short-term economies, when they also know just how cost-effective those services are to them.

Elsa's book therefore comes at a welcome time, with the rapid expansion of higher and further education throwing up many different issues for students and those who teach them. Far from being cocooned in what might seem like the ancient ivory towers of our oldest university, Elsa's experience of counselling in different institutions, together with the pressures on her service at Oxford, as well as her detailed knowledge of the British Association for Counselling, the Association for Student Counselling and the international links with both, all make her the right choice to author a book on counselling in this particular context. In this educational world very little stands still for long, but her book makes an essential contribution to a discussion of the issues today and for many years to come in higher and further education in Britain.

Moira Walker
Michael Jacobs

Preface and acknowledgements

Writing this book has been very much like being a student again. First, there was great excitement about what would emerge. This was followed by utter despair, wondering if there was anything to say that had not been said before. Deadlines were agreed to but had to be re-negotiated because of my unexpected admission to hospital. Then my mother became seriously ill. I was working on the manuscript while managing a relatively new service, chairing the British Association for Counselling and appearing, on behalf of counselling, on a number of national committees – I was like the student who becomes president of the student union, captains the rowing team, works three nights a week in McDonalds, and then wonders why she is not producing essays to her usual standard.

Through all this, there was the constant presence of the tutor/ editor who, in my fantasy, would never be pleased. In fact, Michael Jacobs proved to be an excellent editor. He knew the boundaries of the task and what was appropriate within the framework of the series, kept me to it and firmly dispensed with my flights of fancy (even when I thought that what I had presented was my most creative and brilliant work!). I am grateful to him for his honest appraisal and for his patience when I disagreed with him.

A number of people were generous with their time and experience, especially in talking about the early development of student counselling. Pat Milner, Ellen Noonan, Gerry Rebuck and Brian Thorne gave me access to written material and to their memories, and Gabrielle Syme regularly sent me information she unearthed as she researched her own book in this series. Alex Coren, Craig McDevitt and Ann Heyno have allowed me to use substantial illustrations of their casework. Chris Payne and Val Spargo made sure that I was updated on developments in further education. The staff of Oxford University Counselling Service gave unfailing support and coped admirably with the days when I was somewhat preoccupied and frustrated. Lenore Humphreys and Chris Read rescued me when I was in a panic about the computer, and Chris and Sarah Styles patiently dealt with the numerous drafts of the manuscript.

The case illustrations are based on real people, but identifying features have been removed. In some cases, the personal context or information in sessions is so linked with process that it is impossible to disguise. In these cases, permission has been given for the detail to be produced. Many students and colleagues have allowed me to learn with them during the years I have been a counsellor. To them, and particularly to those who recognize themselves within this book, I shall always be grateful.

Many people have given me personal support. I would like in particular to thank Craig McDevitt and Gabrielle Syme, who convinced me that I could carry on when external and personal circumstances made me think I should give up; Jan Davies who as a long-standing friend and mature student, at the time I was writing, kept me in touch with the student perspective; Eileen Smith, who came in like the cavalry towards the end to make sure that I finished; and Alex Coren, who is a constant support in my work.

· ONE ·

The development of counselling in further and higher education

Searching for the source of student counselling is a little like searching for the source of a river with many tributaries. It would be so much more convenient for the cartographer if there were one fountainhead from which the river rises. Instead, there are a number of springs, some breaking through apparently arid land and others appearing in more fertile soil. Each of these sources, from its unique location, has contributed to the clearly definable river that can be discerned with the establishment of the Association for Student Counselling (ASC) in 1970. Those influences, to a greater or lesser degree, are still found in the Association in the 1990s and in the practice of student counselling throughout Britain.

In 1993, the British Association for Counselling (BAC) carried out a survey of its members and asked them to describe their theoretical orientations. To no-one's surprise, the two most cited models were psychodynamic and person-centred counselling. The members of ASC contributed to this survey and, if we are to trust the art of market research, then we must assume that the balance of theoretical models among the members of ASC mirrors closely that seen among the membership of BAC as a whole. Indeed, ASC conferences in the late 1980s and early 1990s, where the issue of theoretical orientation was firmly on the agenda, demonstrated a loyal – and, at times, partisan – following for these two models. There were calls for attention to be given to those who saw themselves within a more broadly defined humanistic approach, rather than simply person-centred, but it was to be these two orientations which dominated the debate. That these two models were major tributaries to the main stream of student counselling was, and is, beyond doubt. Some would say that they are, indeed, the twin fountainheads – the sources – of modern-day practice. What is most interesting is how these models, significant in counselling as a whole, made their appearance in student counselling.

The development of the models has been dependent on those who practise. To trace the application of these models in the early days is to identify the many individuals who, often unknown to each other, were attempting to introduce their perceptions of a need for student counselling within the institutions in which they worked. By selecting one or two of these individuals as representing the early developments we can begin to see how practice and theory evolved in this setting.

There would appear to be three main sources of influence:

- those who came from psychoanalysis or analytic psychotherapy;
- specific individuals within student health provision in the UK who, although not themselves qualified as counsellors, were convinced of the importance of counselling for students and were prepared to lobby on behalf of its development;
- the North American influence through the model of Carl Rogers and the development of personal counselling in American universities.

PSYCHOANALYTIC/PSYCHODYNAMIC PRACTITIONERS

Mary Swainson

As early as 1934, Mary Swainson, who was then a lecturer in geography (Swainson 1977), was developing an interest in the process of learning and, more particularly, in those aspects of being a student that made it difficult for learning to take place. Her subsequent training in child psychology, which introduced her to play therapy, deepened this interest and, during a period at Exeter Child Guidance Clinic, she began personal analysis with Dr S.H. Foulkes (later of the Institute of Group Analysis). This was followed by a period of Freudian and then Jungian analysis. Her work and personal experience of analysis prepared her for the point in 1945 when she began to apply what she had learned to students.

It is interesting to modern practitioners that this pioneer of student counselling – who had, by today's understanding, a classical foundation in psychoanalytic theory and practice – began working with students in the area of study skills. Implicit in her work was the understanding that effective study skills are based as much on the quality of the relationship between student and teacher or between student and student as in the imparting of a series of techniques.

In 1948, she was appointed lecturer in educational psychology and geography method at the then University College at Leicester, and it was there under the mentorship of Professor J.W. (Billy) Tibble that she began to develop the formal individual counselling that was eventually to become the highly regarded counselling service of Leicester University.

Her description of the process of setting up the Psychological Advisory Service has all the elements that we would recognize today: her own and a few other colleagues' excitement in and commitment to what she was doing; the necessary support from at least one person in a position of influence and power; the reluctant acceptance of her work by some colleagues and the outright hostility and suspicion of others who saw the service as an encroachment on their territory; her tenacity in presenting the service in a way that showed its relevance to the main task of the institution and which ultimately convinced the majority of her colleagues of the usefulness of its existence. One paragraph in her account of the first seven years of her work sums up her feelings and those of some of her colleagues, as she unwittingly played into their suspicions of what she might be doing behind her closed door.

> During the first few years I carried on the teaching work for which I had been appointed and kept as quiet as possible about the rest. At first, counselling had to be done in a tiny room possessing only two hard chairs which I shared with a colleague. However, as we were then a small and self-contained department, the authorities kept moving us; soon I was given a very pleasant larger room to myself in an extension of the old building which (because it used to be a mental asylum) we called the 'luniversity'. This room was big enough to contain a couch, and there is a nice story about this. After my own analysis and training at Exeter (where a couch was a normal item of furniture) neither I nor Billy thought there would be any problem when I asked him to requisition one for the use of those students (or staff – who were now beginning to use the Service) if they needed to relax. We were surprised by the resulting alarm. The principal, Mr. F.L. Attenborough, finally said, 'Well, I don't want the idea to spread, but I *suppose* it's all right with Dr. Swainson?' I wasn't quite sure how to take that one! Anyway, the couch arrived, and by that time it was I who needed to relax.
>
> (Swainson 1977: 51)

Although acknowledging some influence by Carl Rogers, Mary Swainson's work with her students was firmly within the psycho-analytic tradition. She understood her students – and herself in relation to her students – through a firm belief in the power of the unconscious and its various manifestations in the students' inner and outer worlds. She saw this demonstrated in the therapeutic relationship and in the students' practice as teachers. From the beginning she saw herself not just as a therapist but as an educator, with a role to inform thinking on those qualities and structures that would allow for the healthy development of teachers. She did not confine her insights to the counselling room and her many papers and lectures give evidence of her influence – not just in Britain, but throughout the world.

Until 1964, Mary Swainson worked on her own, gradually doing less formal teaching but nevertheless carrying out a dual role within her institution. Sometimes she was assisted by trainees from the course which she had developed. Eventually, after great difficulty in persuading the various authorities and recording '(once more I had to put Billy in an awkward position)', Tony Grainger was appointed to a formal part-time post. Thus we see a now familiar pattern beginning to emerge.

Swainson was a highly professional and experienced practitioner who constantly felt overwhelmed. Although she used her influence and her increasing credibility within the college to argue her case, she was nevertheless dependent on Professor Tibble being put in a difficult situation before her request for extra staff was granted. She was indeed fortunate to have the personal support, and support for her case, of someone who was convinced of the value of counselling and who was prepared to find himself at odds with his colleagues at the highest levels of institutional management. However, despite the increasing credibility of the service, she did not receive personal promotion in terms of her salary and she remained on the basic lecturer grade. Nevertheless, as her teaching commitment gradually decreased, she felt fortunate that she remained on academic conditions of service.

In 1967, she joined the Area Student Health Service, which served not only the university but also the then Leicester Polytechnic and the City of Leicester College of Education. She clearly felt at home there and was warmly welcomed. She records, just prior to the move:

I was trained in a balanced team which included psychiatrists, psychologists, psychiatric social workers and clerical staff. Despite

Dr. Turner's [the consultant psychiatrist] invaluable support for the more severe cases I have felt very cut off during all these years, particularly where adequate medical coverage and understanding at the general practitioner level were concerned, and I shall value the mutual aid and team work more than I can say.

(Swainson 1977: 106)

This merger with the student health service was a pattern that was repeated in a number of institutions at that time, although by 1994, of the 152 institutions that responded to the ASC's annual survey, only four were located within student health services. This parallels the change in thinking from seeing students in emotional or psychological difficulties as people who are ill, to seeing them as those who may well be undergoing normal developmental difficulties. During Mary Swainson's time with the Leicester Health Service, the only way that students could make an appointment with her was by first seeing a doctor. This still prevails in a small minority of services (e.g. the University of London's Central Institutions' Health Service). However, it is much more usual now for students to have open access to counselling services. This has major implications for the practice within these services and for the continued relationship with medical practitioners.

In 1972, Mary Swainson retired and was succeeded by Michael Jacobs, also appointed on a lecturer grade. She continued to offer clinical supervision to a number of student counsellors and her influence is still felt in the 1990s. Jean Clarke, who in 1970 was appointed as the first counsellor at the then Leicester Polytechnic, speaks of the unfailing support she received from Mary Swainson, which clearly stood her in good stead both in her clinical and institutional understanding. De Montfort University, as it is now called, boasts one of the best-resourced counselling services in the country and its staff has, over many years, been influential in the development of student counselling.

Ellen Noonan and the Diploma in Student Counselling at the University of London

In 1972, the first in-service course for student counsellors began at London University (Malleson 1972a). For five years, the University of London's Central Institutions' Health Service had been running a course entitled 'The management of student problems', aimed specifically at people who were in dual roles; people who were academics, chaplains, student advisers, hostel wardens and who wanted to increase their understanding and skill in the management of student problems. This course, run jointly with the University of London's Department of Extra-Mural Studies, regularly attracted sixty people or so to its afternoon lecture. Afterwards, about twenty-five people joined a small seminar group in the late afternoon or evening. The course, although now smaller and called 'Learning and personal development' and run jointly by Birkbeck College (now the home for the Department of Extra-Mural Studies) and the University of Westminster, still attracts the same range of people who are not counsellors but who wish to reflect upon their experience of helping students.

At the other end of the scale, the Central Institutions' Health Service had been running an in-service support group for fully trained counsellors and psychotherapists who were working in further and higher education. The weekly group was led by an analyst, Dr Gerald Wooster, and was paid for mostly by the members' colleges.

The new certificate course for student counsellors was designed to bridge the gap between these two aspects of the Central Institutions' Health Service's educational work. It was recognized that many people practising personal counselling had come to it through informal routes and that there was a need to offer formal training that would lead to a university award. At that time, there were a number of full-time university courses offering qualifications in guidance and counselling (e.g. Reading and Keele), and a full-time course had begun at the University of Aston in 1971 aimed specifically at student counselling. However, London's course was to be the first to recognize that many of those already engaged in counselling work could not devote a whole year to full-time study. The person appointed to run the course was Ellen Noonan.

After taking a degree in literature in her native North America, Ellen Noonan came to London and studied for a degree in psychology. She began working as a clinical psychologist in 1967 in the Young People's Counselling Service at the Tavistock Clinic. This service was set up to offer four sessions, either as a finite piece of work or as an introduction to longer-term counselling. She was also a member of the group at the Tavistock working on career development and institutional thought. This, together with her increasing interest, from a psychoanalytic perspective, in how organizations develop and how people within organizations function, prepared her for organizing and teaching a course whose members would already be practising within an organizational setting.

Shortly after the course began, she took up a part-time post as senior counsellor at City University in London, thus informing her teaching with practical experience within a setting similar to that of the students on her course. This commitment to the concept of the combination of practical experience and theoretical insight has been central to Ellen Noonan's work and one that has influenced the many students she has trained.

Ellen Noonan was one of the early members of ASC and contributed to its pioneering thinking on accreditation and training courses and, on ASC's behalf, became a member of the Standards and Ethics Committee of BAC. Her degree in literature ensures that her thinking is precise and that her writing style is accessible and a pleasure to read. Her first book, *Counselling Young People* (1983), is required reading for anyone involved in the field. This background in literature is important not just because it has enriched her writing and teaching style, but because it demonstrates the diversity of routes by which people came, and still come, into student counselling. At a conference in Bordeaux in 1993, she said that she felt she had learned more about human development from her study of literature than she had in her subsequent training. The rich and diverse backgrounds of student counsellors in Britain is almost unique within the wider European context and may be one that British counsellors will have to defend in the future (see Chapter 6).

Initially, the certificate course in student counselling comprised a one-half day session each week for two years. It soon developed into a one-day a week diploma with an optional, additional third year of advanced study. The third year comprised a placement in a student counselling setting with attention being paid not just to clinical work, but to an understanding of the service within an organizational framework. It is this emphasis on the organization which has given the course a dimension rarely seen in other counselling training. From the beginning, there was also a commitment to the course itself being studied as an organization. A residential week has always been part of the course, the purpose of which has also been to further the course members' understanding of groups within an organizational context. With permission in 1994 to upgrade the course to an MSc, in conjunction with the parallel courses in adult counselling now being run in the same department, the organizational aspect has been preserved and extended. The third year of the MSc programme allows students to specialize in either clinical or organizational work.

This course has made a unique contribution to the development of student counselling. Although Ellen Noonan gave up her day-to-day involvement when she became director of the range of counselling courses within the Department of Extra Mural Studies, the course, organized by Ann Heyno since 1989, still comprises those features which help to prepare graduates for managerial posts within counselling. It is not a coincidence that a large number of heads of services have been members of this course. The fact that three of the four most recent Chairs of ASC have been graduates of the diploma might be seen as further evidence that the course gives people confidence to take on roles on behalf of counselling in demanding settings.

Although this organizational dimension is important, it is not the only aspect of the course important for the development of student counselling. From its uncompromisingly psychodynamic perspective, it has extended the thinking on counselling within the world of education. Because of its specific focus, it has allowed its members and staff to begin to develop an expertise and understanding which they have been able to share with colleagues through papers at conferences, supervision and training. The course itself is designed so that participants can reflect on their own experience of being a student, both in the past and in the present. Each part, including the examination process, gives members an opportunity to be, and then to think about being, a student. This then in turn informs practice in the employing institution. The course still attracts and encourages those who do not wish to become full-time counsellors but who have a counselling component within their roles. Since the late 1980s, it has been the only course specifically devoted to student counselling in Britain. Both Ellen Noonan and Ann Heyno have advised on the development of training for student counsellors in recent years in Denmark, Germany, Italy and The Netherlands. It would appear, therefore, that the course will continue to be influential.

THE BRITISH STUDENT HEALTH SERVICE

The first student health service was established at Edinburgh University in 1930 (Read 1974), with most universities following suit by the early 1950s. These services were developed at a time when there was a clear distinction in the minds of the public, and thus administrators and academics, between the body and the mind. The role of physicians was to ensure that students were physically fit; anything else was considered to be the province of educators or religious advisers. In fact, until the mid-1940s, medical provision was very much confined to detection, prevention and the promotion of physical fitness. Treatment most often took place outside the universities. With the development of the National Health Service (NHS), the assumption was even greater that university students did not require exceptional health services. This, however, began to be challenged by practitioners and the need for treatment as well as prevention was constantly under debate. Mental health issues added an extra dimension to the argument.

Read (1974) notes that in the USA psychiatrists had been appointed to the staff of the health services of Yale and Michigan Universities as early as 1925 and 1930, respectively. Their role was mainly advisory, with cases requiring prolonged treatment being referred elsewhere. Professionals with the label 'mental hygienists and counsellors' also helped with problems that were not of a medical nature. At the time of Read's appointment as psychiatric adviser to the London School of Economics in 1952, he found it difficult to locate others with a similar role in universities throughout Britain, which he attributed to the 'traditional reticence [of the British] about anything in the region of mental derangement'. In 1951, however, a number of physicians and psychiatrists working in university settings had formed the British Student Health Association (BSHA). Their desire to expand the medical model to include a psychological understanding of student problems was given impetus by a report published in the same year by Parnell (1951), which recorded that over one per cent of Oxford undergraduates missed at least one term's work because of psychiatric illness. Lucas (1978) records that this report 'of a suicide rate allegedly eleven times that of the general population of comparable age evoked shock, surprise, and a welter of doubts and conflicting explanations'. Some of the explanations offered came from members of the new BSHA, who had developed an interest in analytic psychotherapy. They were prepared to challenge the traditional view that psychiatric illness was entirely organically based. They were also prepared to challenge their academic colleagues who persisted in the view, that not only can the body and mind be separated when dealing with students and their problems, but also that the educational and the emotional can be easily differentiated by having separate academic and moral tutors.

The BSHA has throughout its development held this tension within its structure and in its meetings. Conference material throughout the years indicates the attention given to both mainstream medical and psychological issues. Subjects such as rubella vaccinations and the incidence of glandular fever in the student population stand alongside papers on working therapeutically with adult survivors of sexual abuse. The burgeoning belief in 1951 that symptoms could be understood in terms of process as well as description was given support by the first international conference on student mental health at Princeton University in 1956 (Funkenstein 1956), where the psychoanalyst Erik Erikson suggested that student problems could be looked at within a psychological developmental model which would have implications for appropriate treatment. The BSHA itself devoted its conference in 1968 to the subject of depression in students, where Donald Winnicott was one of the main speakers. This acceptance of the need for a psychological understanding was again demonstrated by Holdsworth in his presidential address at the 1994 conference of the renamed British Association of Health Services in Higher Education. He urged members to look at their own psychological needs as well as those of their students.

This early work to establish the validity of a psychological approach to students' problems was instrumental in preparing the way for modern student counselling. The doctors involved had the authority to convey their ideas and challenge received thinking. Later, in the 1960s and early 1970s, they supported the increasing demands of academics and students for the appointment of counsellors. However, while welcoming the advent of counselling in higher education, Payne (1978) also expressed concern that it had contributed to the demise of the psychiatrist/psychotherapist as a full-time member of university health teams. He acknowledged that students with psychological problems should not have to present as being ill and in need of a doctor, but he also suggested that there was an important role for psychiatrists as consultants to counsellors. In some universities this was already the case, with physicians, medical psychotherapists and non-medical counsellors and psychotherapists meeting on a regular basis to share expertise and support. In the 1990s, this opportunity for shared work has diminished and some of the implications of this will be looked at in Chapter 5.

While at such universities as Sussex and Leicester, and the then Lanchester Polytechnic in Coventry, there was support from medical staff for the development of counselling, one individual in particular stands out when considering the history of student counselling in Britain.

Nicolas Malleson

Nick Malleson, a physician and later a psychiatrist, was a true pioneer of student counselling while never himself having trained as a counsellor or psychotherapist. Gerry Rebuck, a friend and colleague, described him as a 'Doctor as educator'. Malleson believed that doctors had a responsibility to increase understanding and to be generous with their knowledge and experience. His mother was a general practitioner who was also one of the founders of the Family Planning Association: we can assume that he learned from the example of his mother that doctors could dare to challenge received wisdom, be innovators and have a real and dynamic relationship with their patients.

Those who knew him, while generous in their praise of his many achievements, often comment that most of his work was accomplished in the 1960s and early 1970s when the climate in universities meant that administrators and managers were open to change. As well as the emergence of powerful student politics, which gave the impression that the face of education would be changed for ever, there was money available to try out new ideas. There is no doubt that Malleson knew how to capitalize on this climate of openness. Indeed, his colleagues remark that he was capable of finding money and support where no-one else would even think to look. However, it is also important to recognize that his first post in student health, as physician-in-charge of the University Health Association at University College London from 1949 to 1959, was at a time when doctors were not expected to comment on the academic performance of their patients. He, however, began to see that academic success was as much dependent on the students' physical and emotional well-being as on any other factor and he was not afraid to make his views known.

In 1960, Malleson was appointed physician-in-charge of what was to become the University of London's Central Institutions' Health Service, a post he held until his death in 1976. Between 1949 and 1976, his contribution to the understanding of student problems can only be described as formidable.

By 1954, Malleson was already writing in *The Lancet* on the subject of distressed students and continued to be a prolific writer on the influence of emotional factors on achievement in university education (e.g. Malleson 1963) and on student wastage in British universities (e.g. Malleson 1972b). He gave evidence to the Robbins Committee in 1963, the report of which was instrumental in expanding the provision of higher education. Perhaps he was most revolutionary in persuading the University of London to set up the Research Unit for Student Problems in 1960, of which he became director. He was also the driving force in setting up the Society for Research into Higher Education in 1964. As Rudd (1978) records, the names on the society's first governing council 'read almost like a roll-call of those who had a serious interest in research in higher education at the time. In addition to Nick, Roy Manley and myself, there were Cyril Bibby, Lionel Elvin, A.H. Halsey, Hilde Himmelweit, Alan Iliffe, Keith Kelsall, John Madge, Graeme Moodie, Claus Moser, John Vaizey, Ethel Venables and Henry Walton'. It was this capacity to capture the attention and involvement of the famous and influential, alongside his commitment to each student in his care, that marked Nick Malleson's contribution to the body of knowledge and practice in the area of student problems.

However accomplished he was at using people in the most powerful of circles, he did this with his students' interests in mind. It was with similar motivation that he was prepared to support the developing world of student counselling. As noted earlier, he was the founder of the certificate course in student counselling at the University of London and was careful, in his politically astute way, to make sure that the advisory committee for this course comprised both those within and without the university who would carry influence. The fact that this course has survived when others have not may be due, in part, to those foundations and to the continued care taken to make sure that they have been firmly embedded in its institution. He also recognized that the increasing numbers of practitioners within student counselling needed to join forces so that their views could be heard. With this in mind, he suggested to Patricia Milner, who was then the counsellor at University College London, that she might consider convening a meeting of student counsellors with a view to forming an association. Although Malleson recognized that it would be inappropriate for him to chair either this meeting or any future association, he was the driving force behind the founding of the Association for Student Counselling. It is interesting to note that Walton (1978), in biographical notes written in a book to commemorate the work of Malleson, mistakenly refers to him as the Chair of ASC. While he never held this position formally, it is evident that he was very much the power behind the Chair and, indeed, a powerful and supporting presence for all who took part in the early development of the Association.

THE NORTH AMERICAN INFLUENCE AND PERSON-CENTRED PRACTITIONERS

While the example of practice in North America was influential on those who were developing a psychodynamic approach to student counselling in Britain (particularly that of Erikson, as noted earlier), the major transatlantic influence has been via the humanistic models of counselling.

Milner (1974) notes that the first course in counsellor education in the USA was held at Harvard University in 1911. In the 1990s, many US universities have highly developed masters and doctoral programmes in counselling and are at the forefront of research as well as practice. Equally importantly in terms of the development of counselling in Britain is the oft-repeated story of how the term 'counsellor' came into popular use. Thorne (1984) notes its use in the 1920s when Carl Rogers, the founder of person-centred therapy, who was practising as a psychologist in the USA, was not allowed to use the term 'psychotherapist', because its use was restricted to medical practitioners. He therefore called his work 'counseling'. One day he was practising as a psychotherapist, then with the advent of licensing the next day he put the title 'counselor' on his door. This early differentiation between the two terms for what many believe to be the same practice continues to cause reverberations in Britain in the 1990s (see Chapter 2). However, Bond (1993) records that it is widely believed in North America that the originator of 'counseling' was Frank Parsons, who in 1908 introduced a 'counseling center' when he founded his Vocation Bureau in Boston. The bureau was developed to offer interviews, testing, information and outreach to a largely immigrant community in that part of Boston. This egalitarian and 'lay' approach (i.e. not attached to medical services) to the offering of 'counsel', with its origins in vocational guidance, together with the more therapeutic concept of counselling emanating from Rogers, represent the major influences on the development of student counselling in Britain.

Immediately after the Second World War, Hans Hoxter, who had undergone personal analysis, became interested in its application to the young people with whom he was working through refugee programmes (the cost of psychoanalysis would have put it beyond the reach of these youngsters). After a period in the USA, he believed that the vocational and personal counselling being offered there might be made more readily available if introduced in a systematic way in Britain. In a style that characterizes his work to this day, he managed to bring together the vice-chancellors of many of the major universities in the hope of convincing them that their students would benefit from the opportunity to think about their personal development.

Hoxter went on to become one of the founder members of BAC and the founder and President of the International Round Table for the Advancement of Counselling (IRTAC). He seems consistently to have managed to draw together those who have the power not just to influence, but also to implement. In 1993, he instituted an IRTAC conference in Bordeaux on guidance and counselling in European universities in an express attempt to influence the European Rectors' (vice-chancellors) Conference, which he knew would take place in Barcelona the following year. He managed to attract to the Bordeaux conference a number of vice-chancellors whose active participation in the conference would ensure that its message would not go unnoticed in Barcelona. As he planned, and worked to achieve, the topic of guidance and counselling was placed firmly on the agenda of the Barcelona conference and, under the umbrella of IRTAC, a head of counselling from a British university and the director of the central information service for university careers services in Britain took part in a formal presentation. This modern-day example of his tenacity in getting the twin activities of counselling and guidance on to the agenda is evidence of his continuing influence. It shows, also, how important that first meeting with vice-chancellors must have been in preparing the way for, and establishing the development of, counselling in education in Britain.

By the 1960s, the US influence was more obvious and direct. For example, courses set up at Keele and Reading universities were very much based on the North American model of guidance and counselling as intertwined activities underpinned by a person-centred approach. Courses such as these were supported by Fulbright scholars from the USA, who as professors in counselling were in a position to influence in a fundamental way the curriculum and practice. Equally important was that individuals such as Audrey Newsome had studied for a Master's degree in counselling in North America and returned to Britain with firm views of how counselling should be implemented. Keele University – and the work of its Appointments and Counselling Service, for which Newsome was responsible – was already being described in 1973 as 'the only university in the country to operate a comprehensive counselling service for its own students staffed by counsellors who see themselves primarily as educators and only secondarily as therapeutic resource persons' (Newsome et al. 1973). The practitioners in this service emphasized the desirability of having a single unit to deal with educational, vocational, social, personal and emotional problems. Thorne (1985) later recorded that this philosophy did not always endear the Keele service to other practitioners, who were concerned to develop their identities as professional careers advisers or counsellors. Nevertheless, the assumption that careers guidance is more than the placement of students into jobs and that counselling in educational settings is more than therapeutic work with individuals has been a major influence. There are only a small number of university services in the country which, in 1995, operate in this truly integrated way; however, the 'integrated' student services provision (see Chapter 2) in the former polytechnics and in colleges of further education are testament to this early pioneering work.

Patricia Milner

In many ways, Pat Milner typifies not just humanistic practitioners, but also the many student counsellors who developed their role in a gradual way. In 1963, she was a teacher of history and English in Gosport's first comprehensive school. She described to me recently how she observed the distress caused by the transformation of three schools into one much larger establishment where few felt at home, and where 'teachers were locking themselves into cupboards'. At first, in an informal way, she began to create a space for colleagues and pupils to express their concerns. As her work became more formalized, she recognized her need for training and was supported by her school to attend the one-year Diploma in Educational Guidance at Reading University. Two years later, after having returned to her school, she felt she needed still further training and became a Fulbright Scholar at the State University of New York at Buffalo, where she had what she describes as 'an eclectic training' on the Master's course in counselling.

She had mixed feelings about her time in the USA. While welcoming the opportunity to delve more deeply into some of the theoretical approaches in counselling and enjoying the company of enthusiastic and generous people, her first feeling was one of disappointment (Milner 1970). She felt that the guidance services that she visited were largely an administrative expediency, where the needs of the school came first. Gradually her disappointment waned as she began to realize that what she had been taught by the visiting US professors at Reading was an ideal: 'We had spent a hard, soul searching year at Reading learning about a Utopian fantasy! I am no longer so disappointed, the Americans have not achieved their dream, and we shall not do so either but at least let us start from where they are now and learn from their mistakes' (ibid.). With this realistic attitude she returned to work in Britain.

In 1969, Milner began counselling at University College London (UCL). The post she filled had been advertised as 'Student Adviser' and was to replace the post of 'Tutor to Women'. (It is interesting to note that the view at UCL at this time was that the notion of a special tutor for women was outmoded.) Milner determined from the beginning that the post should be renamed 'counsellor' and knew that she had the support of the Students' Union in this quest. However, she admits that she never quite convinced a large proportion of her academic colleagues that what she was doing was counselling, even when many were referring students to her and recognizing the content of her work. That she was, in fact, practising as a counsellor is evident in the way that students recounted the impact of their work together and the quality of the relationship they perceived to be on offer (Milner 1974).

Milner was supported in her work by the well-established student health service, then under the leadership of Dr Chris Lucas. The service included medical and lay psychotherapists within its team and Pat Milner was invited to attend their weekly team meeting and case discussion. She speaks of learning a great deal from their analytic perspective, although at first she felt it to be foreign territory. They, in turn, learned to appreciate her way of working and began to refer students to her.

Milner speaks warmly of her six years at UCL, but thinks she may have behaved intemperately when she left. She had been lobbying for extra help but could not convince the institution of the need, and therefore felt that she had no option but to look for another post. This story is familiar even in the 1990s. The ambiguity of her role at the time of her appointment has been shared by many practitioners who, like her, have earned credibility through their work. Yet they find it impossible to move their academic colleagues from a position of ambivalence towards counselling, especially at a time when more resources are required, to one where the reality of the work is accepted at an institutional level. It is impossible to know whether she was, indeed, being intemperate in refusing to stay. She may simply have recognized reality once again, and seen that the dream could not be realized in her time.

After becoming a lecturer in education at Goldsmiths' College, University of London, she undertook a lecture tour on counselling in education at South African universities. She later became tutor to counselling courses at South West London College and a freelance counsellor and consultant. Even in her retirement she has continued to contribute to counselling by being features editor of *Counselling*, the journal of BAC.

This editorial work illustrates a parallel theme in Milner's work within counselling. Not only was she a respected practitioner, she was also the founding editor of *The Counsellor* in 1970, the journal of the National Association of Educational Counsellors, and her book, *Counselling in Education* (1974), has informed the work of many who have come into counselling. Most significantly in the development of student counselling as a professional activity, she was the first Chair of ASC.

THE DEVELOPMENT OF A PROFESSION

Of the four examples given to represent the various strands in the development of student counselling, all of them were within the university sector and three were London based. This is not to suggest that development has been restricted to these particular areas. It is true to say, however, that counselling first became formalized within universities, and that the combined influence of various people at UCL and the University of London's Central Institutions' Health Service had a considerable impact on the organizing of student counselling into a professional framework.

During the 1960s and 1970s, with the rapid expansion of the higher education sector, institutions also became more expansive in their provision. The new polytechnics and universities, in line with the philosophy of the time, began to see their work as much more student-centred than had been the case in the more established universities. They also knew that to attract students they had to offer better facilities than the older universities. Furthermore, many members of staff at these new institutions had come from schools and industry, where they had experienced the benefits to individuals of personal attention. It would be inaccurate, however, to suggest that all members of academic staff were in favour of – or had even thought about – formal student support services, but such services were created in most of the new polytechnics. This period saw the greatest expansion in recognized posts for student counsellors.

The development of counselling in further education is much more difficult to trace. This is because, in general, these posts were introduced gradually over many years. Typically, they arose when someone who had been teaching took on some counselling work and managed to persuade the college of its benefits. Another route was through welfare provision, with accommodation or welfare officers expanding their counselling role. In many instances, job titles did not change even if the activity did. In the 1960s and 1970s, many student services officers within the Inner London Education Authority's (ILEA) further education colleges and art schools had substantial training in counselling and viewed counselling as their main role. By requiring applicants to these posts to have had counselling training, colleges presumably recognized and gave their support to such work, without changing the job's title. Thus a hidden cohort of counsellors developed. While most colleges recognized that a qualification in counselling or counselling skills was necessary, even when the posts were weighted more towards other welfare activities, some colleges did not. In the late 1970s, one advertisement for a student services officer suggested that no particular qualifications were necessary but that the person appointed needed to be a 'pearl beyond great price'. It would have been interesting to see how, with the developing equal opportunities policy within ILEA, the interview panel managed to test for those particular qualities!

Although more formal counselling services were set up in some further education colleges, the counsellors were assumed to carry out a multiplicity of tasks. Kirby (1974), in writing about the organization of counselling in North Nottinghamshire College of Further Education, saw a counsellor's function as having four components: (1) educational guidance, including psychometric testing to help determine potential; (2) vocational guidance, with the student's future career as the focus; (3) personal counselling, dealing in a confidential way with 'ongoing guidance with emotional difficulties, unwanted pregnancies, drug experimentation and financial worries'; and (4) liaison with allied services, whereby the maximum amount of confidential assistance would be quickly obtained on behalf of the students.

In the early days of student counselling, many counsellors in further education were members of the National Association of Educational Counsellors (NAEC), founded in 1966 by graduates of the Keele and Reading diploma courses. Since the majority of course members were teachers seconded by their education authorities, the NAEC reflected that membership and their preoccupations. Peter Smart, who was the Chair of the NAEC in 1970, wrote of his concerns after attending one conference, concerns shared by many in all sectors of counselling in education and which would still find an echo today:

> Yet in all this approval I detected a new threat, a feeling of bandwagons beginning to roll, counselling was becoming the 'in-thing' and no matter how unprepared the school organization was, a counsellor would prove the panacea – even if untrained.

On another conference he commented:

> Once again I was worried by the casual approach to the need for training of counsellors by those who advocate expansion.

Heads who were prepared to 'groom' their own counsellors from existing staff, ministers of religion who felt that theological training was sufficient, and others who were prepared to be thrust into the job with no training whatever were present and in some cases reacted rather violently to my plea for a fully qualified counselling service.

(Smart 1970: 15)

Although the situation has not entirely been remedied in the 1990s, it has been alleviated by the increasing public understanding of the nature of counselling and the subsequent concern expressed in the media about the potential damage caused by untrained counselling practitioners. The position in further and higher education has also been helped by the constant lobbying by ASC, which by its annual general meeting (AGM) in 1995 had 740 members, and where for the first time the majority came from the further education sector.

The Association for Student Counselling

In May 1970, Pat Milner brought together representatives from the various areas of higher and further education to present their views on the proposal to form an association of people working in the field of counselling with students. Consideration was given to the existence of the National Association of Educational Counsellors and the possibility of forming a branch for student counselling under its auspices. It was also noted that the British Student Health Association had among its members several student counsellors, and that forming a sub-section for such people would encourage a close liaison between health services and counsellors. A more radical idea was the creation of an association for counsellors working with young people in any setting, whether education, youth work or community service. In addition, it was noted that the Standing Conference for the Advancement of Counselling (later to become the British Association for Counselling) was developing under the auspices of the National Council for Social Services (eventually BAC became an umbrella organization fostering national and cross-sector representation). After discussion of these possibilities, it was agreed that there was a need for a separate and identifiable organization for those in the already existing work of student counselling, although it was also agreed that close links with NAEC and the BSHA should be forged. It was suggested that the next step would be to advertise an open meeting to launch the Association for Student

Counselling, which would then elect a steering committee to carry forward the proposal.

The open meeting was held in November 1970 and was listed in the *Times Educational Supplement*. Of the 114 people invited, 45 attended the meeting (ASC archives). A number of comments were received in writing, among them letters from people at fourteen colleges and universities expressing their support for the formation of an association. Two letters expressed uncertainty as to whether there was such a need at that time.

Much that was to preoccupy ASC in the years to come was voiced at that first meeting. Some attendees wanted an exclusive organization that would meet the needs of those already qualified and practising in formal counselling roles; others saw the benefits of wider links with those who used counselling skills as an adjunct to their primary task. The issue of the relationship between counselling and psychotherapy was raised, as was the notion of counselling being a discipline in its own right. Some expressed the concern that ASC should not be dominated by doctors. Others held the view that the Association should become powerful enough to influence training or even to offer training in its own right. There was also continued confusion regarding the potential role and status of the developing umbrella organization for counselling. But most contentious of all was the proposed membership of ASC.

Although some wanted a broad organization encompassing those already in counselling posts besides those who were interested in and would support the development of student counselling, others wanted a restricted membership. Some suggested that there should be two categories of membership indicating level of qualification: one for 'properly qualified' counsellors and another for 'lay' members. It was also suggested that the lay membership category should disappear once there were enough courses available for members to become 'properly qualified'. Some also believed that membership should be restricted to individuals in universities and colleges of education, because it was felt that it would be difficult for any association to have an impact on salaries and conditions of service beyond those areas, as the provision in further education was diverse and the salary structure was unclear.

Finally, it was proposed by Claude Palmer of Barnet College of Further Education and seconded by Gordon Miller of the Institute of Education in London, that the association should have the provisional title of the Association for Student Counselling and that it should be open to anyone who was engaged in counselling in further and higher education. The proposal was carried and a steering committee was elected with the power to co-opt. It is interesting to note that, despite earlier proposals for an exclusive membership, the steering committee represented the full range of institutions in further and higher education in which student counselling was practised.

This call for exclusivity is not surprising. Since 1969, Audrey Newsome of Keele had been organizing summer conferences with the intention of supporting counsellors already in post. Pat Given, who worked in three universities during her student counselling career, recalls how important these meetings were. She describes how, at every educational conference, counsellors were subjected to suspicious and even hostile questioning by others. She remembers the relief she felt in meeting other counsellors and gaining support from those who understood the setting in which she worked.

It is easy to imagine the sense of loss that some of these counsellors would have felt at the prospect of a larger organization where the opportunity for peer support might be more difficult to find. However, it took a number of years until ASC was able to cope with allowing a division into sectoral groups without feeling that this would result in a divided ASC.

In 1986, at the AGM of ASC, it was agreed to set up a Further Education Sub-committee in recognition of the particular needs of those who worked in the sector. In June 1990, the first informal meeting of Heads of University Counselling Services (HUCS) was convened. A little like the old summer conferences, it was seen as a place for a small group of people to meet and gain support. With the entry of the polytechnics into the university sector in 1993, this group became a larger and less intimate body and found the need to develop a more formal structure. At the 1995 AGM, a resolution was passed to change the constitution of ASC to allow for the establishment of interest groups and thus allow the HUCS group to become incorporated into the ASC structure. It was also noted that the Further Education Sub-committee had completed one of its tasks; that is, to establish the needs of further education counsellors within ASC. Its next task was to reach outwards in order to influence policy makers. ASC has stuck firmly to the proposition in 1970 that it should be an association for counselling and not just counsellors, but it has taken 25 years for the different needs of its members to be legitimized within the constitution.

Pat Milner remained Chair of ASC for six years and was followed by Brian Thorne. During its first nine years, the aims of ASC began to be realized. Not only did its members work hard to define the nature of their work and promote the Association nationally, but a

number of supportive and diligent senior academics and administrators put a lot of energy into ensuring that counselling was recognized in their various institutions. In addition, student bodies
were calling for more trained counsellors. Having discussed counselling at its 1969 conference, the National Union of Students (NUS)
passed a motion calling for the appointment of trained professional
counsellors at its 1974 conference. Thorne (1985) records an extract
from the resolution and comments on the shrewdness of the proposal:

> Conference urges that counselling services should be set up in
> each institution on the following basis:
>
> 1 Staff working in these services should be fully trained.
> 2 The services should be seen as an integral part of the educa-
>   tional programme complementary to teaching.
> 3 Services should not merely tackle individual problems as they
>   arise but should look constructively at ways in which they
>   can (a) adapt institutions, (b) improve learning situations, (c)
>   help individuals to take proper advantage of the opportuni-
>   ties available to them, so that the typical manifestations of
>   student problems do not occur.

In 1979, the cause of student counselling in further education
was greatly helped by the publication of a booklet entitled *Student
Counselling* by the National Association of Teachers in Further and
Higher Education (NATFHE), the union to which most staff in further education colleges and the polytechnics belonged. This publication called for comprehensive arrangements for student counselling,
involving teachers and professionally trained staff. It also recommended a counsellor to student ratio of 1:750, an ideal that has
never been achieved, even in the best-resourced units.

In this climate of support – which might be envied by practitioners in the 1990s – members of ASC saw their work beginning to
flourish and turned their attention to ensuring that they could meet
these external demands for professionally qualified and competent
counsellors. ASC's Training Committee in the late 1970s, which
was chaired by Gloria Goldman of Brunel University, undertook an
extensive review of current training. By visitation and by paper
consultation, the committee sought to determine how far the established courses were relevant to student counselling. This prepared
the way for later work in the 1980s, when ASC published its *Guide
to Training Courses*. This document described the essential and desirable features of training for student counsellors and invited course
leaders to show how far they met these criteria. Updated versions

of the guide have been published and it formed the basis for the 'Recognition of Courses' scheme within BAC.

Some were keen that ASC should itself become a training organization and they developed a series of in-service programmes for its members. Wyn Bramley (University College London), John Morton Smith (Hatfield Polytechnic), Ellen Noonan (University of London Extra-Mural Department) and Bernard Ratigan (Loughborough University) were central to this work, which at first was met with general approval and enthusiastic attendance. However, by 1980, ASC acknowledged that attendance at these programmes had declined. The reasons put forward for this included a better trained membership, a lack of finance and general fatigue. From that time, ASC has confined itself to offering workshops and training during the three days of its AGM and conference. In 1995, the conference was attended by a record number of people (approximately 170), indicating that there remains a demand (if limited) for specific training in the areas of work in which student counsellors are engaged.

It was in the development of its accreditation scheme between 1976 and 1979 that ASC did most to establish the profession of student counselling and, indeed, to influence the profession of counselling as a whole. The scheme, which defined appropriate training, experience and supervision, also insisted on renewal on a regular basis. By its acceptance at the AGM in 1979, the membership was establishing criteria that would make ASC the guardian of the profession. With minor modifications, the procedure for accreditation remains the same today as when first adopted at the 1970 meeting. Its standards are clear but not unattainable and have done much to improve the quality of practice. However, the scheme is also pragmatic. From time to time there are calls for the number of hours of supervision in relation to client contact hours to be increased. Experienced counsellors know that with the rapid turnover of clients in this setting, the close monitoring of work is vital. However, they also recognize that to increase the element of compulsory supervision would potentially alienate institutions which have, however reluctantly, allowed counsellors the time and finances for supervision. So ASC attempts to maintain a fine balance between what is professionally desirable and what is acceptable to the institutions in which counsellors work. When a student counselling post is advertised today there is almost always a reference to eligibility for accreditation with ASC.

In 1983, BAC based its accreditation scheme on the ASC scheme, as well as on work done in the same area by the Association for Pastoral Care and Counselling. The relationship between ASC and

BAC was, for a long period, one of ambivalence. ASC saw itself as a senior organization, but nevertheless wanted BAC to have credibility as a national organization. Thorne (1985) recounts the difficulties he encountered when becoming Chair of ASC in 1976, when the issue of whether ASC should join the newly formed BAC was being debated. Many believed that the cause of counselling would be better served by a national organization that embraced all the emerging branches of counselling, that this larger body would carry more weight with government bodies and attract finance in a way that a smaller and specific organization would not be able to do. They felt that the wider body would be able to raise counselling standards in general, and that this would have a beneficial effect on student counselling in particular. Others were violently opposed to such a move and felt that the work they had been engaged in to develop standards of training and practice would be undermined by belonging to an umbrella organization for anyone interested in counselling, however limited their training. In October 1976 an Extraordinary General Meeting of ASC was called to debate the issue. This meeting which continued all day Thorne describes as 'a painful and tense occasion'; but by the end of the day agreement was eventually reached on negotiating entry into BAC. ASC thus brought its commitment to in-service training and accreditation to this new organization, of which it became one of the first divisions.

The memory of this difficult decision has remained with many of the membership in the 1990s although now, hopefully, in a less powerful way. Some Executive Council members resigned over the matter and others left the Association in protest. Those who remained were determined that BAC should work towards the highest standards possible and that members of ASC should be active in the process. It is perhaps difficult for present and new members of BAC and ASC to understand the legacy of the decision made in the 1970s. For example, the fact that ASC was the last division to hand over its accounting to BAC in the early 1990s was a puzzle to a number of the BAC Management Committee, who could see that ASC would save money and that it would make BAC accounting more efficient. When the treasurer of ASC announced at the 1995 AGM that the Executive had finally agreed to BAC Finance Office handling the day-to-day accounting of the Association, he was careful to add that all cheques had to bear his signature. While many of the earlier anxieties and suspicions have been alleviated because of BAC's commitment to promoting and monitoring professional standards, as well as to supporting those who have an interest in counselling, the membership of ASC prefers to retain as much autonomy as possible. This will provide another interesting area of debate with the development of the UK Register for Counsellors (Chapter 6), which is based legally and financially within BAC. ASC will have to negotiate the status of its accreditation scheme within the register, and thus a lively debate for the second half of the 1990s is ensured.

During the 1980s and early 1990s, ASC has built on the work of its first members. In the mid-1980s an Advisory Committee to Institutions was formed, producing a widely distributed publication which sets out conditions of service, appropriate salary levels and the range of activities in which counsellors might be expected to engage. This committee is constantly used by members who wish, or are compelled, to enter negotiation with their institutions on the manner of their work. It has also been called on by university and college authorities to mediate when difficulties have arisen between managers and their employee counsellors. While ASC has never set out, nor presumed itself, to be a trade union, many of its members have had cause to be grateful for the sensitive way in which the Advisory Committee has conducted itself since its formation.

Other committees developed to support the work of the membership include the Research, Press and Publicity Committee and, most recently, the European Sub-committee. All of this work is carried out by volunteer members of ASC and, as in many other branches of counselling, dependence on volunteers in the 1990s is becoming a problem. ASC has been fortunate during its development that institutions have allowed members time and resources to carry out its work. With cost-centre accountancy in the ascendancy in the employing institutions, the real cost of running ASC has come to the surface. In 1994, for the first time, the AGM was informed of the difficulty of appointing a new Chair. The amount of time required to carry out these duties meant that potential candidates felt that they could not guarantee the support of their institutions. An acting Chair was appointed while the Association consulted its membership about raising fees in order to recompense the service from which future Chairs might come. They also undertook to review the structure of the management of the Association. These difficulties, in an association and division of BAC which has had a high profile and is financially sound, have major implications for those who wish to see counselling continuing to develop as a professional activity in the second half of the 1990s and into the next century.

CONCLUSION

From the outset, those who have been engaged in the practice of student counselling have been careful to make sure that it is safe, appropriate and professional. Many have seen themselves as 'voices crying in the wilderness' as they have attempted to attract the resources necessary for the task. Such is the experience of those whose lone voices bring a new and, at times, uncomfortable message to established institutions. However, since the days of Mary Swainson, Ellen Noonan, Nick Malleson and Pat Milner, practitioners have received support from each other and from others who, while not trained as counsellors, have been sympathetic to their work. It has been this capacity to come out of a necessarily isolated position, in large and sometimes hostile organizations, and to spot the fertile soil where it exists, that has marked out the practitioners and services whose work has flourished. This needs to be borne in mind by those who practise in the 1990s and by those who take on responsibility for the further development of the profession. As we shall see in the next chapter, the 1990s have provided their own challenges to the practice of student counselling: the need to be alert to the changing political and private context and to the opportunities within them; the need to collaborate with those who share a belief in the value of the work; the need to make the work open and accessible. All of these are just as important as they were when the pioneers of student counselling first staked out the land and recognized the possibilities for growth.

· TWO ·

Counselling in further and higher education

Studying the history and development of an organization poses questions as to what has changed and what remains a perennial issue. It is most likely that the pioneers of student counselling would recognize many of the problems and opportunities faced by modern practitioners. In order to understand the practice of counselling in the 1990s and how the profession has changed, it is necessary to put modern work in its context, and to clarify present definitions of the task.

THE CONTEXT

The early 1990s saw considerable change in the structure of post-compulsory education in Britain. No sooner had the polytechnics become corporate bodies and removed themselves from the charge of the local education authorities (LEAs), than the government decided that they might call themselves universities. The most quoted reason for this was that the quality of graduates from the polytechnics was in many cases as high as that from the universities. Employers, however, seemed not to have heard this message and continued to discriminate in favour of university students at the point of recruitment: polytechnic students were disadvantaged by their status. So overnight, polytechnic directors, who had only just got used to calling themselves chief executives, became vice-chancellors, and the students became university students.

Next it was the turn of the further education (FE) colleges, which were also removed from the local authority structure and became corporate bodies responsible for their own financing. Advertisements for chief executives of these colleges appeared in the educational press alongside those for what were once assistant principals, newly designated as directors of forward planning or marketing, or some such appropriately business-like name.

It could be argued that institutions of further and higher education needed to respond to changing times and changing populations, and that they needed to become more efficient. That these changes have affected the nature of the student experience is certain. External change has implications for the internal world of the student. It is natural and appropriate at points of change to experience anxiety and excitement at one and the same time. If there is a sense of consistency in the outside world, then changes in the internal world can be managed successfully. When the external world mirrors the uncertainty of the internal world, then anxiety can become unmanageable for some and the need for counselling services increases.

A counsellor in a further education college was puzzled by the theme of aimlessness which was appearing in different guises in his work with students. He knew, as an experienced counsellor, that students often expressed a need for clear boundaries, but during the preceding few months client after client seemed to be expressing anger or despair that no-one seemed to care enough about them. Others were feeling lost in their work and could not see the purpose in what they were doing. Students who had been regular in keeping their appointments began to miss sessions or to arrive late and there seemed to be more illness around than he could ever remember. When he took time to reflect on the process as well as the content of his work, he began to see that the students were expressing something of the context in which they were studying. There had been a change in director. The management systems had been restructured. Staff had been uncertain about their futures and the future of the institution. This had in turn affected the students, who were unable to see the links but who had felt the impact of uncertainty. They had turned the institution's anxiety into their own and had arrived at the counselling service convinced that there was something within themselves that needed to change, that they were personally and solely at fault for feeling purposeless or angry or afraid.

The immediacy of the sense of change in the early 1990s may reduce as the decade comes to a close, but the product of these changes and what institutions have become will have a lasting effect on the student population. In the mid-1990s, there is concern that the adoption of the terminology and the culture of the world of business has led to a less personal – a more mass-produced – form of education, and that those who have responsibility for management forget that businesses do best when attention is paid to the needs and development of the workforce. While this is not the appropriate place to offer a critique of the rationale, philosophy and practice behind these changes, the fact that they are occurring creates a specific context within which students and counsellors work and therefore needs to be acknowledged. People have come to realize that a change in name does not always guarantee a change in status, and students who feel themselves to be products with a brand name stamped on their foreheads are apt to feel that their personal contributions have been neglected – that is, the packaging is more important than the content.

THE CLIENT POPULATION

Further education

It is important to understand how and why students enter further education, because the way in which it is done may influence their experience of education and may be the underlying reason why some make their way to a counselling service.

When young people reach the age of sixteen and the end of compulsory education, some are given the choice of staying on at, or leaving school. Staying on at school has traditionally meant opting for a course of study that is fundamentally academic in content, rather than vocationally based, and has always been seen as the prerogative of more able students. Indeed, many schools demand a defined number of passes at specific grades at General Certificate of Secondary Education (GCSE) level, or 'Lowers' in Scotland, before the student is allowed to study for Advanced level GCSEs or Highers. This is still the case in most schools, even with the gradual introduction of more vocationally based courses. But what of those young people who do not consider themselves clever enough, or are told that they are not clever enough, to stay at school? And what of those who feel that they have outgrown the structure and atmosphere of school life? What are the options for them?

What is clear is that employment is not a real option. Sixteen-year-olds are no longer employed as their parents were. The apprenticeship schemes which for many youngsters were an initiation into adult life and the world of work have long since disappeared. Some young people opt for government training schemes, designed to provide experience of work and offer training for a limited period of time, in addition to providing a small financial incentive. Others opt to do nothing at all, becoming financially dependent on their parents, as they are not entitled to claim state benefits. At the same time, because their children are no longer attending school and therefore not deemed to be 'children' any more, the parents lose their Child Benefit payments from the state. It is within this curious and ambiguous context – not a child yet still dependent – that adolescents are expected to develop psychologically and make decisions about the next stage in their lives.

For many the ambiguity is tolerable and indeed may not be a conscious part of their decision making. Some wish to continue their education, albeit not at school, and in a limited number of areas nationally they are able to opt for a sixth-form college. Most well-motivated young people who do not wish to stay on at school find that their only option is to join an FE college, where there is a wide range of subjects on offer in what they perceive to be a more 'grown up' atmosphere. However, there are some youngsters who opt for an FE college – those who would have preferred to find a job, or who had begun a training scheme but were unable to sustain their interest – simply because they can think of nothing else to do. FE colleges thus find themselves in the position of catering for a large number of young people who are at an important stage in their adolescent development but who have many different wishes and expectations. Readers can decide for themselves whether this is an enviable or unenviable task. However, this is only part of the picture.

FE colleges have developed out of the old technical colleges where, traditionally, apprentices and trainees attended on a day-release basis to gain the certificates and diplomas that would consolidate their vocational training. This practice can still be seen today in the 'off the job' training offered by colleges for those individuals on training schemes sponsored by their 'employers'. In parallel with these schemes are the numerous part-time courses offered to those in employment who wish to further their career development. For some it is a requirement of their job that they attend these courses. Others persuade their employers that their performance will be enhanced by enrolling on such a course. This is an important opportunity for learning which some embrace enthusiastically, whereas others see it as a chore to be endured in order to remain in employment. While these courses may be important for the student and

are an essential aspect of the drive to educate the working population of this country, the importance to the college should not be
underestimated. This is where the money is made. This is the means
by which lecturers' and even counsellors' jobs can be secured, for
while FE colleges receive most of their finances via the Further
Education Funding Council, they are dependent on these more
commercial activities for their survival.

What is less well known is the range of courses now offered to
students of all ages who enter FE colleges via a route other than
school or employment. FE colleges have an important role to play
in making education accessible to those who in the past would
never have believed they could, or would be allowed, to study. In
a typical FE college today, the courses on offer are of a variety of
lengths, levels and structures. They are geared towards, for example, those who have had a less than positive experience of education in the past; those who are unemployed and who need to
acquire basic skills in literacy and numeracy; those who have never
been in paid employment, such as single parents and women who
until this point have cared for children and homes; those who are
temporarily unemployed and who need to retrain or increase their
skills; those of retirement age who are finding enjoyment and ful-
filment in this third age of study.

The courses that have had a fundamental effect on counselling
services in further education are the 'Access' courses, developed to
prepare students without traditional qualifications who wish to enter
higher education. These courses allow young and often older adults
to test their capabilities for study, build skills, improve their understanding of the subject material and, perhaps most importantly of
all, develop confidence in their 'academic' selves.

Some Access courses end with a traditional examination, but more
usually an assessment of the student is made based on records of
achievement and what has come to be known as 'profiling'. This
requires that the student takes an active part in self-assessment and
that the lecturer and student negotiate the final grade or comment
on achievement. Many see this as a real advance in methods of
assessment. Self-assessment does indeed require the student to
engage with the experience of learning and can change long-held
perceptions of how learning takes place. Students are often asked to
write a personal learning history. In addition to being a journal of
learning on the present course, the students are asked to identify
their earlier learning experiences. Such a process, when handled
well by the lecturers responsible for these courses, help students to
recognize the skills that they have acquired through life experience.

Allowing students to trace their learning histories also allows them to gain a deeper perception of themselves and increases their expectation of what it is possible to learn about themselves. This opening up of personal experience can bring students to counselling services with very sophisticated demands and needs to explore these new perceptions and to gain further insight. Even on the best courses, however, this process can produce much personal confusion and often leads to a need for formal counselling. At worst, on courses where there is little understanding or recognition of the impact of these practices, students can feel exposed to unmanageable feelings about themselves and their histories, and they can arrive at a college counselling service in great personal crisis.

FE colleges are developing ways of challenging the notions of how people learn and who can learn. On the one hand, they demonstrate the most progressive aspects of education in Britain; on the other, there are still some bastions of old-style teaching where the lecturers remember formal classes with young apprentices kept in check by staff who had learned their trades during military service. It is even possible to find both these ways of working in the same college, with all the tensions that this produces for staff and students.

It is also important to consider the physical environment in which the students study. By opening up colleges and making them more accessible, many have truly become 'community colleges'. By providing a welcoming atmosphere, pleasant surroundings and the feeling that everyone has the right to learn, such colleges afford comfort to those taking up new opportunities and challenges. Elsewhere, the notion of accessibility has created its own problems. It is not unusual, particularly in inner-city areas, for FE colleges to have highly sophisticated and potentially intimidating security systems, installed to discourage those who wish access but not access to learning. One London FE college has a barrier at each entrance, which can be opened by the use of a security pass only, and guards with Alsatians on duty throughout the day as well as at night. At this college, the counsellors were asked at one point to patrol within the college to identify troubled youngsters (who were legitimately inside the security system) at the point where they were causing trouble. It was difficult to convince the management group, who saw this as a necessary and benign activity, that what was really needed was a team of detached youth workers to work with these disaffected young people, rather than lone counsellors acting as trouble-shooters. Although this is an extreme case, at the Association for Student Counselling's AGM in 1993, a motion that drew attention to the increased number of highly disturbed people being admitted into FE colleges called for increased psychiatric support.

So the context of further education is complex and the client population is varied. At one end of the spectrum are courses in very basic skills; at the other are courses which are highly academic in nature and, indeed, an increasing number of colleges now offer courses at degree level validated by universities. Thus at this end of the spectrum the boundaries between further and higher education are becoming more diffuse. Students may be highly motivated and successful or they may be unmotivated and, despite the best efforts of the college, may be consolidating their experience of failure with all the pain and personal anxiety that that entails. Most will be somewhere in the middle, sharing moments of achievement and, if not moments of failure, moments of fearing failure. Any of these students can and do find their way to counselling services.

Higher education

Entry into higher education in Britain is highly competitive and selective, which may come as a surprise to student counsellors in those countries where there is a constitutional right to enter university. The impact of this selection procedure is fundamental, in that this atmosphere of competition is central to and continuous throughout the career of students and can be a major influence on the views students have of themselves and their capacity for study. Although some students are able to thrive and are motivated to succeed in such an atmosphere, others are less at ease and can be disabled by their conscious and unconscious responses to what they perceive as the cost of achievement. Alex Coren, writing in the *Oxford Magazine* (the internal journal of Oxford University), quotes a very bright student, who said that the trouble with being clever is that you can never be clever enough.

Application to university is through a central clearing system, whereby potential students fill in a form a year in advance on which they list a limited number of universities in order of preference. When and if they are offered a place, they are allowed to hold up to four firm offers until the results of their examinations are known, which can create enormous anxiety among the students (and their parents and teachers). The minimum requirement for entrance is two grade E passes at A level, although in practice most courses ask for more, and the level at which the entry grade is set is determined by the level of demand for the course. It is not unusual for medical faculties to ask for two passes at grade A and one at grade B; indeed, some consistently demand three A grades.

> A medical student was referred for counselling because, contrary to the expectations of his tutors, he had failed his first year examinations. He described how his first-choice university had demanded three grade As at A level. He was so furious at what he saw as a ridiculous demand that he determined to put them in their place. He studied hard and achieved the requisite number of grade As and then accepted a place at a rival medical school that had been less stringent in its demands. Now at this second medical school he seemed determined to deprive the profession of his undoubted skills by failing. Although there were many other complicated issues which had to be addressed in the counselling sessions, the rage at what he felt to be the arrogance and elitism of a profession that he had wished to join from childhood, and which he saw as essentially there to do good in the world, had to be explored.

Some universities accept alternative entrance qualifications, including a Business and Technical Education Council (BTEC) higher national diploma, which, as its name suggests, is more vocationally based, or a General National Vocational Qualification (GNVQ). While there is some acceptance of these qualifications as alternatives to A levels, most academics view them with deep suspicion. Mature students (i.e. those aged over twenty-one years) can gain admission without any of these formal qualifications, providing that they can prove to the university's satisfaction that they are capable of studying at undergraduate level. It is at this point that the profiles developed at FE colleges may be considered or, for mature students coming straight into higher education from work or unemployment, a scheme which formally acknowledges that learning can be carried out in less formal settings (Accreditation of Prior Learning) may be used. Though most potential students find this flexibility reassuring, others may feel that they have already failed because they have not arrived via the 'normal' route. They may feel that they have been given special dispensation and have failed to prove themselves. One consequence of this is that they may be over-anxious about their performance and their right to be in higher education. They thus continually attempt to prove to themselves, their tutors and their peers that not only are they as good as the other students, but better than them. While for some this is an enabling and motivating dynamic, for others it results in considerable distress and the need for intensive and often lengthy counselling.

Some students opt to apply to colleges of higher education (HE) where the entry requirements are usually lower than for university (although this is not always the case). HE colleges offer courses similar to those made available at the old polytechnics and, indeed, were poised to be designated polytechnics when the polytechnics became universities. Many HE colleges grew out of smaller institutions, such as teacher training colleges, and offer a wide range of courses to degree level and beyond. Because of their flexibility in catering for part-time students and their industry-related activities, they are often the first choice of mature students returning to study.

Most undergraduate courses leading to a Bachelor's degree take three years to complete, though some take four. Some courses combine three years of study with one year of industrial placement or, in the case of foreign languages, a year abroad. In Scotland, where there is recognition of the need for the first year of undergraduate study to be a foundation and transitional year, it is normal for the degree course to last four years. However, the government is encouraging institutions to introduce accelerated two-year degree courses. Most academics and students are firmly against this idea, seeing the potential for much more pressure. They also argue that for learning to have real value, time is needed for the subject material to be integrated and reflected upon. However, some students (in particular mature students) welcome this initiative, as they see the opportunity for reducing their period of dependency and, more importantly, financial hardship.

This illustrates the profound debate concerning the nature and value of university education. On the one hand, there are those who argue that universities are purely for the pursuit and enjoyment of knowledge. Others hold that universities should be entirely functional, preparing students for employment as efficiently and as speedily as possible. Others have a more pragmatic view and, while attempting to develop courses that allow for personal interest and educational growth, also structure them with at least one eye focused on the potential for employment. These conflicting views are played out in senior common rooms, at meetings of university committees and at the highest level of political engagement. They are also played out in the lives of students, who may find themselves confused, struggling to find a sense of purpose in their studies.

Those who choose to continue their studies beyond undergraduate level will again face fierce competition for the places and funding available. British university education is distinct from that in

most other European countries in that, despite the increasing preoccupation with vocational qualifications, the belief still prevails
that an undergraduate degree will prepare an individual for employment no matter how obscure the subject covered and no matter how seemingly unrelated it may be to the profession or vocation
to be followed later. It is therefore not unusual for an historian to
become an accountant, or a chemist a lawyer. It is the postgraduate
training in these cases that is the deciding factor. Traditionally, this
training has taken place 'on the job', with diplomas being undertaken full-time at professional institutes or part-time at FE and HE
institutions. A small number of students go on to study for a Master's degree and an even smaller number continue to doctoral level
in order to obtain a PhD. Funding for these higher degrees is limited
and the competition for places is fierce. The classification of undergraduate degree (1st, 2:1, 2:2 or 3rd) obtained will determine a
student's capacity to obtain employment or a place for further study.
A 2:1 or occasionally a 2:2 used to be sufficient for students to be
accepted for a further degree, but today counsellors see students
who are anxious about the need to get not just a 1st but a good 1st.
Counsellors no longer see this merely as a manifestation of some
long held and unresolved rivalrous conflict but recognize the reality
in the anxiety. Ironically, these much prized places on higher degrees
are no more a guarantee of employment than the clutch of GCSEs
or A levels held by school leavers. University counselling services
see many students who despair that, despite their doctorate and the
high regard in which they are held within their field, there are few
posts – even of a temporary nature – for which they can apply.

> A young woman was approaching the end of her
> undergraduate studies. During her time at the university,
> she had attended the counselling service in an attempt to
> deal with her lack of confidence and her inability to enjoy
> university life. She was the first person in her family to
> have attended university and, coming from a working-class
> background, she had found the language and culture of the
> university foreign and alienating. Now at the end of her
> course, she had returned to the Service asking for help to
> decide about her future.
>   Despite her earlier difficulties, she had done well on the
> course and in the final year had undertaken a piece of
> research which had confirmed her tutors' view that she was
> an outstanding student. They had told her that she was
> certain to obtain a 1st and were so convinced of the

originality of her research and, if further developed, its potential impact on the politics of a troubled country, that they had already sought funding for her entry on to Master's degree with guarantee of further funding for a PhD. She had also been offered a job with a top accountancy firm.

While the need to make a decision had to some extent reawakened her earlier conflicts about her right to be at university and her acceptance of her academic self, the main focus of her anxiety was the certainty of life as an accountant against an uncertain future as an academic. For although funding for the further degrees was assured, her tutors agreed that there was no guarantee of paid employment at the end. For a working-class woman whose father had been made redundant while she had been at university, the choice seemed almost unbearable.

While this young woman could be viewed as being in a very privileged position and to some extent the focus of considerable envy, her dilemma illustrates the risk taken when someone commits themselves to continued education at whatever level. They are being asked to invest their talents and enterprise, to delay the sense of reward, and to trust that their investment will pay dividends. To a student population only too aware of the sudden collapse of large financial institutions, the risk of keeping all their investment in one place may provoke enormous and realistic anxiety.

So far, we have looked only at the complexities of entering higher education and the anxieties that may be aroused. For some, the process of getting there is an all-consuming activity which leaves little energy for being there. Unfortunately, some students never feel they reach their academic potential nor their capacity to enjoy student life. One twenty-year-old said in counselling, 'It's as if I reached my peak at A level. It was a golden time. Things will never be the same again.' However, whether a student arrives at higher education exhausted by the process or full of life and exhilarated by the challenge, they will soon discover that they have entered a complicated institution where many more choices are to be made, both academically and personally.

The traditional view of universities, where one subject is studied in depth for the duration of the course, is much cherished, particularly in the older universities. However, modularization is now in vogue. This entails students picking modules, that is discrete courses which are usually of one term's study (or, more recently, a semester, which can vary in length but typically crosses the time span of the traditional term). For the duration of the degree, students mix and match modules to create their own, personalized degree. The advantages are clear if one is committed to the principle of self-directed learning; the idea that one learns best when what is being studied is seen to have relevance. However, it leaves many students unsure of what they should be studying. This system calls for a strong tutorial and guidance structure in order to help them choose wisely. However, tutorial time is being cut in most universities and it is often departmental secretaries who find themselves telling students that the preferred module cannot be pursued because it clashes on the timetable with another module they have already chosen. Other modules are offered and often they are appropriate since secretaries tend to know their courses and their students well. However, too often they are inappropriate and offered simply to ensure that the student is studying something somewhere at the appointed time. Many students thrive in such a system, appreciating the sense of autonomy and purposefulness. Others, however, do not and they find their way to the counselling service feeling lost and with a lack of self-esteem. They find the system does not allow for sustained contact with specific academic staff and for relationships to be developed wherein difficulties can be explored. In Chapter 5, the importance of the tutorial system and its relationship to counselling is described in more detail, but here it is appropriate to note that the increasing complexity within the systems of further and higher education calls for an equally sophisticated and well-resourced structure of support. The waiting lists at some counselling services attest to the absence of such support.

Examinations

It is axiomatic that examinations are part of the context within which students and student counsellors work. The effects of examinations on students' psychological well-being and on the practice of counsellors will be outlined in Chapter 4. However, to really understand student counselling, the significance of examinations throughout the entire academic career of a student has to be appreciated.

From the moment students enter university or college, they focus on the ending and the result they will achieve. Although at many institutions there has been a move away from the traditional three-hour examination at the end of a course to a system of continuous assessment, this has not necessarily lessened the anxiety felt by students. Indeed, many supporters of the old system maintain that continuous assessment equates with continuous pressure and that students never have the time to relax and enjoy the course, or to pursue a line of interesting thought if it is not part of the designated assignment. Although some students revel in the motivating anxiety in the build-up to examinations, others become paralysed with fear. What cannot be denied is the constant feeling of being tested. This is an identifying theme in the practice of student counselling, so it is not a surprise that the most frequent opening sentence in a first session is 'I can't work'. Despite the often rarefied debates on the purpose of education and the role of a student, many (including students) believe that the only function of a student is to pass examinations. If they fail in that, then they cease to exist.

This description of further and higher education as a context for counselling is inevitably brief and, perhaps, over-simplified. Little attention has been given to the other side of the student experience, which is often enjoyable and fulfilling. One of the burdens of student counsellors is that, when they appear in public in their institutions, they often feel like 'Cassandras' – they only come out when the news is bad! The preceding paragraphs may give the impression that there is no good news and that everything is problematic. The reality is that counsellors tend to see only about 4 per cent of the student population (ASC 1995). Even allowing for the general under-provision of services and the fact that some troubled students always choose to find help elsewhere, we must assume that the majority of students negotiate the system successfully and even enjoy themselves.

Education is competitive, taxing and challenging, and often produces great uncertainty. It is in a state of change and this change affects students and their capacity to study. It is subject to outside influences, which seem to challenge the very nature of the idea and ideal of student life. It is unrecognizable to the student of the 1960s and early 1970s, when education seemed to be a passport to independence and individual exploration. The pressure now is to conform and to aim for the security of settled employment as quickly as possible. Some may consider this no bad thing. However, in conforming out of anxiety, students are missing the opportunity to try out new identities from which creative thoughts may emerge. Regular conference attenders who sleep in rooms in university halls of residence vacated by students will have noticed that the posters left on the walls say something significant. The ubiquitous photo of 'Che' Guevara has all but disappeared. In its place they are much more likely to find a poster of Winnie the Pooh. It is as if students dare not even fantasize about changing the world, but must hang on to the comforting images of the past as they face an uncertain future.

Student finance

It is unrealistic to talk about student counselling without paying some attention to the difficulties surrounding student finance. It is a complex issue and complicated in practice.

Students entering higher education are entitled to a mandatory award administered by the LEA and funded through a national system. That is, anyone studying for a BTEC higher national diploma, a degree or other certain designated courses (e.g. specialist music courses), and who has been 'ordinarily resident' in the area for three years, can apply to their LEA for financial support. How much they receive is based on their parents' income, their own income if they have been in employment for three years or are over twenty-one and are thus deemed to be 'independent'. The minimum they receive is payment of fees; the maximum is payment of fees plus a limited maintenance allowance. Students who are lone parents or who have dependants who are not working will receive additional allowances. However, the maintenance allowance is means-tested against disposable income from the previous year. Once that income rises beyond a certain point, then parents are expected to contribute on a sliding scale. What is most controversial is the introduction of a student loan system intended to top up the grant and to be repaid after completion of study. Even with the loan, which many students are reluctant to use, income is now below that which the government decrees as the minimum level of income upon which non-students are expected to survive. Since students cannot claim income support or unemployment benefit during vacations, many are declaring that they can no longer afford to be students. The lack of casual jobs during vacations, which in the past allowed students to manage financially, has contributed to the difficulties. It is ironic that at the same time as the government has expressed a commitment to widening access to higher education, it has made it more difficult for those without considerable financial resources to take up the increased number of places.

The grant system for students in further education is both simpler and more complicated. It is simpler because there is no mandatory entitlement to financial support for anyone over the age of eighteen; therefore, students know where they stand. However, it is more complicated because (1) discretionary awards may be made to the value of the grant for higher education (although these are becoming rare); (2) fees can be paid for some courses and not for others; (3) on some courses it is possible to continue to claim unemployment benefit providing the course is less than twenty-one hours per week and the students declare themselves available for employment; (4) there are different entitlements for lone parents, refugees, etc.; (5) while under-eighteens continue to receive free education, they are not allowed a maintenance grant unless they come from very low income families and, for example, were given free dinners at school; (6) some younger students may be given a travel allowance dependent on the distance their home is from college. The availability of all of these, apart from statutory state benefits for a very limited number of people, varies according to the wealth and generosity or commitment of the LEA.

The issue of finance is central to all students' sense of security and continued well-being. It is an ever-present concern, even for those from relatively wealthy backgrounds. At the heart of the matter is an ambiguity about status and autonomy. Both those who are struggling to become independent adults, and those who are attempting to rework aspects of their adult life so that they can be more productive, receive a mixed and confused message. At worst, they feel as if they are not valued.

While many of the practical issues relating to finance may be dealt with by other specialist services within the institution, most counselling services (whether they are linked to an advisory service or not) see students who are distressed and angry about their financial status. Although the reality of their situation cannot be ignored, it is interesting to consider why some students manage to survive the experience of being poor without feeling deprived. Counsellors see clients who bring with them the context of their internal worlds as well as the reality of the external world. It is by drawing on their understanding of how personal histories can affect responses to difficulties in the present that counsellors can begin to understand the particular meaning of a problem, shared with other students, but experienced by each student in a specific way.

DEFINITIONS AND THE STRUCTURAL CONTEXT OF COUNSELLING

In Chapter 1, we saw that within the historical development of student counselling in Britain there has always been a link between counselling, guidance, the giving of advice and psychotherapy. Whether there should or should not be a direct link in the performance of these functions is a matter of continued debate.

For many years, counsellors have been attempting to define their role in a way that both makes sense to the public and does justice to their specialized skills and training. Many have begun by defining what, in their view, counselling is not. They state very forcibly that counsellors never give advice. This is understandable because the verb 'to counsel' is more commonly used by people outside counselling circles when they mean to advise, as in 'I would counsel against that'. Thus counsellors have been faced with two difficulties: (1) the historical understanding within the English language of the verb 'to counsel', and (2) the foreignness of the new concept of counselling. (In Chapter 6, when we look at links with student counselling in other European countries, we will see that this confusion is unlikely to be cleared up.)

While defining themselves in ways that distinguish the activity from advising may have been convenient for counsellors outside education, and may even have become a point of principle, the position inside education is more complicated both in theory and in practice. The debate as to whether or not counselling should be considered to be a discrete and specialized activity is demonstrated by the variety of structures within which counselling is placed in universities and colleges.

The more common practice in the older universities is that counselling is separated from guidance and advice. There is usually nothing in the structure that allows the heads of these various services to communicate other than on a voluntary basis. Reporting tends to be through a pro-vice-chancellor or a management committee to Senate or Council, the governing body of the university. In a small number of the older universities, and in most of the new universities and HE colleges, there is commitment to the idea of integrated student services. Here counselling, careers guidance, accommodation services, financial advice, chaplaincy and sometimes sporting activities operate as discrete functions, but the heads of these units come together on a regular basis to discuss common issues and report through a head of student services to the governing body. In a small number of universities, the functions of giving advice and counselling are contained within the same post; in others, the counselling and advisory service is one unit, but different people perform the functions. Although counselling and advice may be seen to be related, it is rare that counselling and careers guidance are combined in higher education, despite the influence of the Keele model in the early years.

In FE colleges, the same variety of structures can be found and there has been a similar increase in the number of integrated student services. This is a relatively new phenomenon and is as much the product of colleges' need to sell themselves to potential students as a belief in the necessity of student support. It is now recognized that the colleges which can present a 'customer care package' will be more likely to recruit and retain students. An interesting development in some colleges has been the involvement of counsellors and advisers in guidance activities at the point where students join. Here, alongside college tutors, the student services staff help students to be more clear about their reasons for entering further education and what they may need in terms of future development. Guidance is offered about courses of study and the choices that are possible, and the financial implications are explained. Advocates of the combined system of counselling and advice, both in colleges and universities, use this example to demonstrate that personal development and practical choices are so intertwined in the educational setting that to separate them presents an unrealistic and theoretically unsound view of human development. Those who support the system of discrete services argue that it is important to keep the boundaries between the various activities clear, so that students can make a real choice about which of the forms of help they wish to take up.

A large part of the debate about separate or totally integrated services has centred around counsellors' need for professional recognition. This was apparent at the first meeting of ASC and remains the same in the 1990s. However, stances on the issue are often based on prejudice and lack of information about the activities involved. At one extreme there are those who suggest that only 'pure' counselling sessions have any real value. They have a tendency perhaps to look down on those individuals who carry out combined activities. At the other extreme are those administrators who insist that counsellors are being precious and territorial; and there are practitioners in allied fields who claim that they, too, act as counsellors. While this debate has particular relevance in educational settings, since some argue that the whole of education is about guidance and personal development, it is played out elsewhere, as the Differentiation Project (Russell *et al.* 1992), managed by BAC and funded by the Department of Employment, showed.

This report, set up to inform what was then the National Lead Body for Advice Guidance and Counselling, offers confirmation of the premise that counselling should take place when there is a clear contract to engage in the activity and when the boundaries and purpose are made explicit. Thus an adviser or a guidance worker employing advanced counselling skills as an adjunct to the main task is not a counsellor unless the nature of the contract is changed. This confirmation, alongside an understanding that counselling is defined by the permission given to make the internal and emotional work the main focus, has implications for those who occupy a dual role within educational institutions. For unless counsellors make clear what they are offering and allow their clients an opportunity to decide whether or not to engage in the activity, they cannot be said to be functioning as counsellors. The clarity in this definition also has major implications for those managers and administrators who set up these complicated posts.

Many with such mixed roles have found a way of making the contract explicit during sessions that is sensitive and not too heavy-handed. It takes skill to point out to a client that the tenor of the session has changed without interrupting the process and making it difficult for the client to carry on talking. Some counsellors favour a strategy that temporarily halts the process so that the client can make a deliberate choice to continue in the same vein. Even when people come quite deliberately to counselling, they may feel that they have been caught up in the process and leave the session feeling that they have said too much. If students looking for practical advice find that they have unintentionally revealed aspects of the problem which may have been unknown even to themselves, they may feel coerced and manipulated. It is for this reason that many counsellors not only stop mid-session in order to ask a student whether or not they wish to continue with the different focus, but quite specifically point out that the nature of the contract seems to be changing and that the student should make a further appointment at which the counselling process can be made explicit from the outset.

All those who have worked in these multiple roles know that students often test out the approachability of counsellors by bringing a practical problem in the first instance. They may do this two or three times before they can make the real issues known. It is most important that counsellors are aware of what is being asked of them and that they respond in a way that makes boundaries clear, is trustworthy and thus ethical.

A young female counsellor in an FE college was asked by a tutor to see a sixteen-year-old student who was having financial difficulties. As well as counselling, she was responsible for giving advice and information about accommodation, welfare and finance. The tutor said that the student in question was one of the best seen on the course and that they would be sorry to lose him if his financial difficulties could not be resolved.

When the student arrived for the appointment he gave

the impression of being confident, sophisticated and courteous. He said he needed to know whether he was entitled to a travel pass or not. He had moved and was uncertain whether or not he could claim from the new education authority. The counsellor asked whether he had moved with his family, but he responded that he had moved in with his girlfriend. The counsellor was aware that even in this inner-city area it was unusual for someone as young as sixteen to have left home and moved in with his girlfriend, and was concerned that his financial difficulties would not be resolved solely by receiving a travel pass. After some gentle questioning, the student stated that his girlfriend was older than he was and was in employment and so was happy to support him financially, but that he did not like to be entirely dependent on her. He thought that he might leave the course and get a job if he wasn't entitled to a travel pass. In saying this he also expressed some dissatisfaction with the course content and the standard of teaching. As the session developed, the young man revealed that his parents were divorced, that his girlfriend was thirty-three years old and that his father did not approve of the relationship. Each time more information was given the counsellor felt there was still more to come, so she kept the session open, even though she could have quickly answered the travel pass question. Finally, the young man said that his girlfriend, until two months ago, had been his father's long-standing girlfriend.

The counsellor, as even an experienced counsellor might have done, found it hard not to be fascinated by so transparent an acting out of an oedipal conflict. Since this was also beginning to be in evidence in terms of the student's attitude to the course and his male tutors, she had to carefully remind herself of the boundaries of the present relationship. She asked whether the student wanted to talk further about his situation; he replied, that as far as he was concerned, if he could get his travel pass sorted out then everything would be fine. It was five weeks later that he booked an appointment for himself and began by saying, 'I've been thinking about your offer, and I think I would like to talk about my relationship with my father'.

It takes experience to switch roles in a way that is authentic and does not appear alienating to the student. This is not always under-stood by those who are responsible for creating and interviewing for posts where advising and counselling are combined. In higher education, where the discrete counselling function is most often found, a team of counsellors usually allows for less experienced counsellors to learn from colleagues. In FE colleges, there is often only one post with the title of 'counsellor', but within which the person is also expected to take on an advisory role. It is often to these posts which newly qualified counsellors are appointed without administrative and secretarial back-up and with no opportunity to learn from experienced colleagues. The FE sub-committee of ASC has an important function in making sure that these isolated counsellors are linked with other experienced lone practitioners, and with colleges where there is a more extensive and experienced team. However, the responsibility for this should not rest with ASC alone. Managers and administrators need to understand its importance if they have an interest in the quality and safety of provision in their institutions.

It is important to attend to this specific contextual issue in student counselling for two reasons: first, because it is a lively and central debate and, second, because it defines the basis for the chapters that follow. Whenever counselling is described in this book, it is on the assumption that this is an activity consciously and deliberately entered into by both counsellor and client, even when the 'counsellor' has a multiplicity of roles within a particular institution.

The issue of where counselling and psychotherapy overlap, are the same or are different, is as hotly debated as the differences between advice, guidance and counselling. An interesting development in the work of the Lead Body, which has added psychotherapy to its remit since the Differentiation Project was commissioned, has been the emergence of the term 'therapeutic counselling'. This term was coined as the developing standards, and the competencies therein, began to show a difference between what can broadly be described as counselling that is clearly related to a specific situation or a decision that has to be made (i.e. the focus of the counselling is the client in the external world), and that harder to define counselling where complex and deeply held assumptions, which may be out of the client's awareness, are worked with. Both can be found in student counselling and are often carried out by the same practitioner. The term therapeutic counselling has not found favour with those who argue that all counselling is, of itself, therapeutic, but for many it has been a useful working definition of that activity where there is a clear remit to focus on the inner world of the client. It is when counsellors are working in this mode that it becomes difficult to draw clear distinctions between counselling and psychotherapy. What is indisputable is that there are few psychotherapy services in further and higher education. The services are almost all called counselling services. What the institution understands by this and what counsellors believe it gives them permission to do often creates tension in the practice of student counselling. In the following chapters, many examples are given of actual work with students and the kinds of problems they bring. Whether they prove to be examples of counselling or psychotherapy is not at issue in this book. But they are examples of what student counsellors do.

STUDENT COUNSELLORS IN THE WIDER INSTITUTIONAL CONTEXT

Student counsellors may still be refining definitions of their work in ways that are relevant for themselves and their institutions. This is to be expected and is desirable if the profession is to be open to change and remain a dynamic force. The area of institutional work is one of the most defining characteristics of the role of student counsellors.

From its very beginning, ASC stated that a student counsellor should be able to work preventatively and developmentally within the institution as well as with the range of problems presented by individual students. Later, in its *Guide to Training Courses in Counselling* (ASC 1993), where essential and desirable features of training for student counsellors are defined, an understanding of institutional dynamics was included. So while the formal counselling aspect of the work, whether with individuals or in groups, may be private and confidential, the preventative and developmental work is public and much more open to scrutiny. For some counsellors, this poses a problem. Many have chosen to work in counselling because, by nature, they prefer to work quietly and unobtrusively. To discover that they are expected by their Association to take on a more pro-active and public role can be challenging and, for some, unwelcome. This wider work raises the question of counsellor responsibility, as many believe that counsellors should only be responsible to their clients. Others argue that those who work in an institutional setting have a tri-partite responsibility: to the client, to the institution and to themselves. It is within this latter framework that ASC expects its counsellors to operate.

Preventative work

There are many examples of this work throughout the country. Counsellors offer instruction on study skills, groups on anxiety management, pre-examination groups, discussion groups for students who have newly arrived in order to help them settle in, and courses in basic helping skills for students so that they can listen more constructively to colleagues who are troubled. All of these services prepare students for the task of being a student and help to prevent the escalation of problems. By doing this, counsellors contribute in a practical way to the life of the institution by trying to address potential problem areas before they arise. These activities also take counsellors outside their consulting rooms where they are seen by students and staff to be more approachable.

Developmental work

Developmental work is not so easy to define and it is often less easy to convince institutions that such work is appropriate and valuable. It is based on the premise that counsellors are able to make a unique contribution to the culture and development of an institution. Counsellors bring with them a specialist knowledge of student life and are able to indicate ways in which the organization might make the experience of being a student more productive, and ways in which it might already be causing stress and a lack of productivity.

A counsellor noticed that for several years running an unusually large number of students at the beginning of a particular course were coming to the counselling service demonstrating symptoms of anxiety (e.g. psychosomatic complaints and doubts about their competency) and wishing to transfer to other colleges or courses. Because she had already developed a role for herself on the curriculum committee of that course, she was able to give feedback to the course organizers in a way that was both appropriate and non-threatening. The result was that the early part of the course was restructured. The material studied remained the same but the method of introducing it was changed.

Counsellors have a particular view of the educational process and its impact upon students. The skill and subtlety of their work rests on the manner in which they express this view so that the institution is able to understand. It also rests on the way in which they encourage the institution to create a space within its structure so that as counsellors they have a formal route through which they can report and influence developments. This latter task is particularly difficult, not simply because universities and colleges have complex bureaucracies which are difficult to change, but because of the unconscious factors that are at work.

A counselling service is often viewed with great ambivalence by the rest of the institution. Its very existence states that all is not well and that there are problems to be faced. This is not the message organizations wish to hear. Often structures are developed (or not developed) that demonstrate the unconscious desire of the university or college to split off problem areas into a counselling service, which is then expected to remain hidden and silent. If there is no channel through which the service can report, then there is no challenge to the organization to integrate those split off parts and become more complete. The counselling service then becomes a receptacle for sick students, a place where the disturbance of the organization can be deposited.

Viewed from the other side, unless counsellors engage in some of the everyday developmental tasks of the institution, their perceptions will become distorted. If they see only disturbed students, they will begin to see only the disturbed aspects of the institution. Reality is required on both sides if each is to be helped to resist fantasies about how the other operates. However, even when structures are developed to allow counsellors a formal voice within institutions, ambivalence can and does still occur.

Just as individuals who come for counselling can project their fantasies on to the counsellor, so groups and committees can respond to the counselling service in ways which reveal unconscious wishes. Some have the idealized view that the service is wonderful and indispensable; the fantasized hope is that the service will solve all of the organization's problems. Others denigrate the service as useless and inappropriate; they do not value it, because for them it represents the needy aspect of themselves or the organization which they in some ways also despise and would like to be rid of. Others have a more realistic view of what the service can and cannot do, and do not expect the service to be all knowing and all providing. Neither do they fear the service for knowing too much nor accuse it of being withholding.

The danger for counsellors who are the object of unconscious processes within a university or college is that they start to behave as if such fantasies are real. They start to see themselves as the only caring part of the institution and start to behave as if they were some subversive force for change. They may even begin to believe that they should be consulted on all major problem areas, since they are the experts, and become outraged if they are not. Conversely, they may become convinced that nobody in the institution

values anything that they do and can become full of despair. They
may also from time to time need to experience the variety of people, each with their own views, who are also part of the institution,
and thus learn that there are shared hopes and aspirations as well
as shared moments of hopelessness and retreat.

Whenever counsellors are involved in activities other than formal
counselling, they are still seen as representing the counselling service. This can represent the start of the therapeutic process.

A young man, previously unknown to a counselling service,
appeared late one Friday afternoon. He did not have an
appointment but conveyed to the receptionist that he was in
great distress and feeling suicidal. Fortunately, a counsellor
was able to see him almost immediately.

It became clear to the counsellor as the session progressed
that the student was seriously at risk. He had no hope,
could think of no-one who would mourn his death, was
angry with his family and friends, was denigrating of his
course and the people in the university, and had made clear
and definite plans for his death.

Some considerable time into the session, when the
counsellor had made sure that she had conveyed to the
student that she had heard and understood the depths of his
despair, she said that she wondered if his coming to *the
service* meant that he wanted to be stopped from killing
himself. He looked straight at the counsellor and said, 'I
didn't just come to the service. I came to see *you*'.

The counsellor was shocked at the force of this statement
and felt the power of this angry young man, as he appeared
to be demanding that she alone should save him from
death. For a moment she was unable to think clearly, but as
she tuned in again to what the student was saying she
began to understand. 'You see', he said, 'I saw you when
you came to speak at the induction course for new students.
You seemed so different from anyone else that I
remembered you'. When the moment was right the
counsellor said, 'You have come to see me because I, and
what I stand for, represent for you the possibility that there
is a different way of living within this university'. He
replied, 'I suppose I have'.

This powerful example shows how work inside a counselling room
was influenced by the counsellor being involved in the wider activities of the institution. Whether the student would have made his

way to the counselling service without that first impression of the counsellor at the induction programme will never be known. What is clear is that a dynamic relationship had begun without the counsellor knowing. That she was there at all was enough to begin the process.

Although preventative and developmental work has become a distinguishing feature of student counselling, counsellors in this setting still spend most of their time in mainstream therapeutic work and later chapters illustrate the detail of this.

After an initial period of growth in the 1960s and early 1970s, expansion of services came to a halt. Indeed, concern was expressed in the mid-1980s that services were at risk of closure. In his report to the AGM of ASC in 1985, Paul Terry (Chair of ASC), spoke of the many counsellors who were worried that some aspect of their job, or even the service as a whole, was under threat. ASC did not, until the 1990s, record systematically details of national provision, but the minutes of meetings show that, despite worries about services being in jeopardy, most counselling services were able to argue their case and survive. By 1994, all universities apart from Stirling had a formal counselling service, although none had reached the ideal set out by NATFHE (see Chapter 1), nor even the recommended ASC rate of one counsellor to 2000 full-time equivalent students (ASC undated). In further education, there was an increase in the number of fully developed services, although there were still many poorly defined services where people with little training were being expected to perform with inadequate support. Welfare work and teaching commitments remained important for those in further education.

Perhaps the most worrying trend in student counselling in the mid-1990s has been the increase in seriously disturbed students using services. Earlier it was noted that the 1993 AGM of ASC was concerned at the lack of medical support for those dealing with disturbed students, particularly in further education. In order to quantify this concern, ASC asked its members during its annual survey in 1994 whether or not they felt that the number of disturbed students was increasing. Sixty-four per cent of those who responded reported an increase in psychological disturbance; only 2 per cent believed that it had decreased. A number of factors were thought to have contributed to this increase. First are the changes in mental health policies that have meant that more people are expected to be cared for within the community – a number of these people find their way into education, particularly into FE community colleges. Linked to this is the perception that some academic departments, often in the spirit of equal opportunity, have changed their criteria for selection. Third, the increased number of mature students has brought an increase in long-held, even entrenched, problems. Add to this the greater numbers of students whose parents are separated or divorced, who are recounting a history of abuse and who feel under greater pressure to succeed, it is easy to see why counsellors feel that they and their services are under pressure.

Thus in the 1990s, student counselling services are dealing with complex situations and the evermore complex demands of students. Counsellors are expected to work creatively with a wide variety of cases, but many of the issues they face are shared with others in parallel counselling fields. Some of these issues are peculiar to, and even exacerbated by, the particular setting. These similarities and differences are considered in Chapters 3 and 4.

· THREE ·

Common counselling issues

In Chapter 2, attention was given to those factors that influence the practice of student counselling. In this chapter, the focus is on common issues shared with other counsellors, wherever they are practising, where the underlying principles might be the same but where the context has a considerable effect on the nature of the relationship. This calls for a careful understanding and interpretation of the fundamental principles of counselling.

CONFIDENTIALITY

All student counsellors who are members of the Association for Student Counselling (ASC), and therefore also of the British Association for Counselling (BAC), are bound by the BAC Code of Ethics and Practice, which emphasizes the importance of confidentiality. It also makes clear that clients should be informed as to what this means in practice. A number of counselling services, where there is a mixture of professional backgrounds within the team, have chosen to become organizational members of BAC. In doing so, they oblige all team members to abide by the same code of ethics and practice.

Educational institutions have systems, both formal and informal, for sharing information regarding students. This is important because it allows them to monitor and assess students' progress and to become alert to potential problem areas. Faculties within colleges and universities speak proudly of how well they know their students. Some even see themselves as in *loco parentis*, even though this is no longer the case in law. This has a strong influence in terms of how organizations view their relationship with students, including how much they think they should know about students in difficulty. The presence of a counselling service which sticks to a strict code of confidentiality may be seen as a threat to the fundamental ethos of the institution. Counsellors may find it difficult to convince the rest of the institution that they appreciate and are in tune with the aims of the organization, without compromising each student's need for confidentiality.

This situation arises from a basically healthy and proper regard for students' welfare by tutors and teachers, although the desire to know is not always healthy curiosity. Counsellors sometimes have to find a way of working with and educating academic colleagues who have become too involved in students' lives. Sometimes their task is to help colleagues to let go of students without feeling that their role has been usurped by the counsellor.

Conversely, some counsellors hold the concept of confidentiality so dear, refusing to give any information at all about their work, that they engender an atmosphere more akin to secrecy than confidentiality. They also use a spurious commitment to confidentiality as a way of avoiding accountability. In such instances, counsellors begin to find that they, and the services they represent, become the focus of misperceptions and even hostility.

From time to time, all counsellors who work in institutions are faced with reconciling responsibility to the client with that of the employing organization. In particular when young people are involved, this can be complicated by strong emotions and complicated systems of protocol as everyone attempts to 'get it right'. Counsellors need to be clear in their own minds about the issues involved if they are not to be caught up in various forms of institutional anxiety. When an individual student's crisis is not handled carefully, it can often develop into a crisis for the entire institution.

Ellen Noonan writes of two inherent dangers in counselling: first, that the 'room will convert itself into a confessional or a *boudoir* with deleterious consequences for the meaning of the transaction between the counsellor and client' (Noonan 1983: 144). She goes on to identify the dynamics of the confessional as one where the client's desire is for the counsellor magically to absolve or obliterate all that is unpleasant, and where the counsellor may be lured into a sense of omnipotence, including a need to 'observe the sanctity of the confessional'. Alternatively, when counsellor and client behave as if the room were a *boudoir*, they can become excited by the intimacy and exclusiveness of the dynamic. Noonan writes, 'Both the *boudoir* and the confessional occur in a vacuum and ignore the wider reality of the client's life. Sins and secrets, absolution and excitement, are not the business of counselling'(ibid.:145).

If counsellors understand that the basis of counselling is to help students speak about their internal worlds so that they, together, might better understand their response to the external world, then confidentiality provides a safe context in which deeply held fears, desires and thoughts can be expressed and explored. The opportunity to do this in private is of central importance to counselling work. However, since it is also clear that students inhabit real worlds and that others in it have an impact on their lives, then it may be possible to collaborate with those others in a way that is both appropriate and creative. This can be done without revealing precise details of the counselling session. With students' permission, enough information can be given to individuals within the organization with responsibility and concern for students, for them to continue to operate in a way that is both helpful and appropriate to their roles.

A student attended the counselling service after being referred by her GP. She was extremely depressed and unable to work. Her tutors had been contacted by the GP and in the student's perception had changed from being strict and demanding and telling her that she was lazy, to being over-indulgent and telling her that it did not matter if she failed to produce work. Since she had a real understanding that work missed now would be difficult to repeat in time for examinations (she was studying a subject that required timetabled laboratory work), she was confused and did not know what to do. Missing work and letting down her peers in the laboratory was adding to her sense of guilt and thus to her depression. With the student's permission, the counsellor contacted the tutors concerned. She was able to explain that the student needed to be clear about the consequences of not producing work at this time and that to give her this information would be the kindest and most appropriate thing that they could do. As a result of the information then given to her, the student was able to see that she would be unable to attend to her personal needs and her academic responsibilities at the same time. She negotiated with the college to take a year out, during which time she had regular counselling. When she returned to college, although she had not completely recovered, she was well enough to meet the demands of the course.

As a matter of course, most counsellors ask their clients whether or not anyone else knows of the particular difficulty they bring to the session. It is one way of checking if students have support between sessions. When it is clear that their problem has the potential to affect their work, it is straightforward to ask if a tutor knows, and if not, whether the tutor can be told. Part of the counselling process is to work with the response to this suggestion. Invariably students are relieved to have it confirmed that their tutors are interested and concerned about them. The counsellor and student can then work out what can be said and who should take responsibility for conveying such information. In most cases, the student takes the initiative and speaks to the tutor and gives permission for the tutor and counsellor to liaise. Sometimes the counsellor takes on the task in order to prepare the way for the student to speak to the tutor. Either way, it is an opportunity for counsellors to make the work real to other colleagues and to make the institution real to themselves.

The need to be clear about the information to be shared outside counselling is particularly important when dealing with individuals who have referred a student to the counselling service. If someone has been concerned enough to make an appropriate and formal referral, it is at the very least courteous to let that person know, with the student's permission, that the student has attended and that the work has begun. More problematic are informal referrals when a tutor, doctor or adviser suggests to a student that they might profitably visit the counselling service. After a period of time, such students integrate the idea and attend saying that they have referred themselves. Meanwhile the referrer, out of concern, contacts the service to see if the student has taken up the suggestion. Since it is usually a secretary or receptionist who deals with such inquiries, it is important that they are fully briefed by the service, which should have a clear policy on whether or not this kind of information should be divulged in these circumstances. Counsellors working on their own need to be especially clear about their policy on confidentiality, even if the student has never been near the service. It is an informal call, taken between clients and without a secretary to act as a buffer, that can find counsellors off their guard and tempt them to act outside their normal code of practice. One of the first questions to ask an enquirer in this situation is whether they could ask the student themselves, and to take the opportunity to explore any misunderstandings about the nature of information that can be shared. It is possible to allay the fears of referrers that they might be seen to be intrusive or coercive if they make their own enquiries of their student.

This constant process of education about the nature and boundaries of counselling is an intrinsic part of counsellors' work. Knowing what to say, how to say it, and discerning who can cope with what is being said, is an important part of counsellors' own education and development.

Confidentiality and accountability

Educational establishments have become part of the 'contract culture' in which audits and quality assurance are facts of life. Counselling services have not escaped the request for public accountability. In Chapter 6 the broader issues of accountability are raised, but here we address the issue of inspection and assessment within the context of confidentiality.

Until the mid-1980s, counselling services in universities and colleges were by and large left to their own devices. Occasionally, ASC would be informed of the management of an institution questioning the role and effectiveness of its counselling service, but it appeared that there was no systematic monitoring of services. However, two cases that taxed the thinking of the ILEA Association of Student Services Officers, most of whose members had a formal counselling role, and subsequently came to the attention of ASC, are of importance.

In the first case, a principal of an FE college, believing that all files and all work within a college were the property of that college, insisted that a counsellor's files should be made available for inspection by him. He was not prepared to accept that the files contained personal and confidential information. A telephone call to ILEA's legal department by the chair of the Association of Student Service Officers confirmed that all counsellors' files should be confidential unless called for in legal proceedings.

The second case was much more difficult to resolve, and it was not until 1993 that legal opinion clarified the matter. It arose from a visit to a student counselling service by a team of Her Majesty's Inspectors, after an inspector asked to sit in on a counselling session. The counsellor refused and thus began a long and difficult exchange between ASC and the HMI.

It is unfortunate that the latter case arose, because student services units were starting to be included in inspections of FE colleges and polytechnics. With some trepidation, this move had been generally welcomed by counsellors and other student services staff. Their hope was that when the inspectors' report on the institution was published, comments about student services would have to be taken seriously. Inspection also implied a recognition that these services contributed to the central task of the institution (i.e. the furtherance of academic and personal development). Even the request to sit in on the interview was understood to have been made by the inspector within the context of a wish to promote student counselling and prove the efficacy of the work. Given the goodwill on both sides, it was sad that a protracted debate evolved to define the boundaries of confidentiality.

Bond (1993) gives a detailed account of how this issue raised ethical questions for all counsellors. He records that legal opinion had to be sought from counsel in order to resolve the differing views. While this opinion has yet to be tested in the courts, it provides a sound basis upon which counsellors can be confident that their professional judgement in such cases must be given due regard.

ASSESSMENT

In the early years of student counselling, it would have been difficult to identify a procedure for formally assessing prospective clients. Instead, it was done in an informal way as counselling progressed. This was at a time when the demand for counselling services could be met. A student would arrive at the service and be taken on by a counsellor with a free appointment. During the first session, the counsellor would check that the student had come to the right place, for example that this was not a problem that required specialist legal advice. At the same time, the counsellor would look out for any signs of a psychiatric or medical disorder that might require referral. All other assessment criteria were dealt with as the work unfolded and formed part of the counselling process. Some services were based on a model that used the first four sessions for mutual assessment by the client and counsellor, at the end of which agreement was made to proceed or to finish. If the work proceeded, it was often open-ended; clients could have as many sessions as they needed, although usually only one session per week. Sometimes a review was built in at the end of each term, but the general ethos of the work was that student counsellors could deal with almost anyone and anything that came through the door. That was what they were there to do, however long it might take.

This is not to suggest that all students were seen for long periods of time or that counsellors were undisciplined in their approach. In fact, because of their largely adolescent population, where the psychological imperative is independence and autonomy, much of their work was short-term in nature. At a conference on psychotherapy in the university setting at the Tavistock Institute in 1989, counsellors and psychotherapists found that on average nine sessions per client was normal both in Britain and North America. Since that time, the demand for counselling in British institutions has grown without a commensurate growth in the numbers of counsellors. This in particular has forced counsellors to adopt a more formal assessment procedure.

In 1990, only a few counselling services in further and higher education had procedures for an intake assessment session. The counsellors in such services tended to come from a social work or marriage guidance (now RELATE) background, where the intake session was common practice. By 1994, virtually all heads of university counselling services reported assessment procedures in place, and were discussing the ever increasing demand and the problems of what to do with students once they had been assessed. The experience at Oxford University may serve as a useful example of how external forces have forced a change in practice within a short period of time.

In 1989, an expanded counselling service was introduced as a result of a major review within the university. Two of the goals set for the service were that students should be seen for appointment within three days of contact, and that the service should help to prevent students from developing 'inappropriate psychiatric careers'. Those appointed were all experienced student counsellors with a confident view of how a university counselling service should operate.

These counsellors had come from services where it was usual to continue to work with students they themselves had seen for the initial appointment. A modification was immediately introduced, partly to ensure that resources were used appropriately but also as a way of developing an understanding of how each counsellor worked. Students were offered up to four sessions in the first instance. If it was the view of both the counsellor and the student that further counselling would be helpful, then the case was brought to the weekly staff meeting for discussion. In this way, counsellors had the opportunity to check their assessments with their colleagues and by so doing the members of the team became more familiar with each other's practice. Such meetings underlined the principle that the use of resources was something for which each team member had responsibility.

During that first year, demand for counselling increased to such a level that assumptions about familiar practice were challenged. Thus a briefer assessment procedure was introduced. During the first session, the counsellor now looked in particular for any signs that the student might be at risk or that the level of distress was so high that waiting a number of weeks for a further appointment would be seriously detrimental to the student's welfare or that of the university community. Those who were considered to be a priority were now discussed at the weekly staff meeting and decisions about who should offer regular counselling were based on the availability and expertise of the various members of staff. This was the first major change: instead of counsellors continuing to work with students whom they saw at their initial appointment, they had to refer within the service. This had implications not just for the assessment of the nature and intensity of the problem presented, but also for the way counsellors conducted themselves within the initial session with the prospective client. Now they had to help the students to attach themselves to the service rather than to individual counsellors.

As this system developed, another issue emerged which had a negative effect upon team morale and ultimately upon effectiveness. Since all students considered to be a priority were discussed at staff meetings, and because there were at least two or three cases per week, soon this became virtually the sole item on the agenda. There was no space to talk about work that was proceeding well, to make decisions about longer-term work or to discuss other important issues affecting the team. The only topic of discussion was the most difficult work. Since all of these cases presented with strong elements of hopelessness, the unbearable nature of the presenting issues began to worm its way into the operation of the team dynamic. The counsellors were in danger of becoming as traumatized as their clients by the relentlessness and bleakness of the problems that were presented week after week. In order for the team to function again in a more measured way, decisions regarding priority cases were to be taken outside staff meetings.

The next development saw the head and deputy head of the service reading each week the notes of those assessed by counsellors as priority cases. They assigned students to those counsellors who had available time and who would be able to deal with the issue presented. Thus a more traditional managerial approach began to evolve. This was very different from the philosophy that had been evolving within the service, that each counsellor, whether full- or part-time, was considered to have a high degree of autonomy in deciding which cases they could and should deal with. Thus the increase in demand for counselling had an effect not just on individual practice, but on the way that the service was managed.

By the end of the academic year 1990–91, it was clear to those working in the service that however inventive they might be, they were never going to cope satisfactorily with the demand. While a bid for extra staff was wending its way through the various university committees, the service continued with its policy of assessment during the initial interview. Those who were assessed as priority cases were usually seen within a week or two for regular counselling. Those not deemed to be a priority were put on a waiting list. This was far from satisfactory. Since priority cases were by definition the more complicated and pressing, they were also those for whom longer-term counselling was often necessary. Students on the general waiting list, whose needs could also be considered urgent, were waiting for an increasingly long time for regular counselling. The service was turning into one which dealt with only the extremely disturbed or disturbing members of the university community. The consultant psychiatrist shared the counsellors' assessment that, despite the very difficult and distressing stories presented by the priority students, few needed formal psychiatric intervention. The service was therefore meeting one of its stated goals, that students should not develop inappropriate psychiatric careers; but that students should be given regular counselling within three days of their first contact was clearly not being achieved. The two goals seemed incompatible.

By the end of the autumn term in 1992, it was clear that the fifty or so people on the waiting list for general counselling were unlikely to be offered regular counselling for at least three months. Three months is a long time to wait for anyone who is in distress but for a predominantly late adolescent population, where there is such a sense of immediacy, this was an inappropriate waiting time. The fact that undergraduate terms at Oxford University are just eight weeks long added further to the feeling of urgency. The counsellors, too, felt under pressure and feared that they were in danger of behaving unethically by advertising a service that they were unable to provide. Various options were considered: the first was to close the service to new clients until the waiting list could be cleared; another was to restrict the service to undergraduates, since graduate students often seemed to require longer-term counselling; a third was to refer all priority cases to the health services. All these options were rejected and a plan was instigated to allow some assessment of newly distressed students, whatever their academic status, and liaison with the health services and other pastoral services within the university.

When students attended the service, they were dealt with in a clear but gentle fashion by the reception staff. They were told that they would be offered an initial session with a counsellor and that they could be guaranteed at least one follow-up session. If more sessions were required, then the counsellor and student together would decide on the best possible way to proceed given the limited resources. The students were given this information verbally when they first made contact and then in writing when they arrived for their first appointment. What emerged during this period was a learning experience for everyone.

The counsellors found that the pressure on time made them much more active in the process of counselling and that this had a therapeutic effect. It became clear that the initial session could be used not just for assessment, but to address the presenting problem in a substantial way. Where appropriate, this was done by linking past experience or history to a focus in the present and holding this focus in mind throughout. The need to be more active and to engage with the client more readily meant that a working alliance quickly developed. There was a real sense of counsellor and student working together to agree what could be resolved in the limited time available, and what might be left to one side for the time being. The students therefore identified what was and was not tolerable and this allowed them to create some order out of the often chaotic material presented. At a time when they were feeling hopeless and lost, they were able to get back in touch with their capacity to observe and make decisions. At the same time, their feelings of misery and hopelessness were acknowledged and worked with. Even the decision when to hold the follow-up appointment could be used therapeutically. This underlined the counsellors' increasing awareness that each communication during these very brief encounters had many layers of meaning and potential effect.

A female student had been raped by a male student who had formerly been a friend. She had been persuaded by her friends and the college authorities to come to the counselling service some time after the event. The material presented during the initial session showed, as well as the trauma of the immediate incident, considerable ambiguity in her relationships within her family of origin. When asked when she would like her next session, she requested a two- or three-week gap. When her reasons for this were explored, it emerged that she was the one in her family who could cope and that this was repeated during her college life, as she had taken on a responsible and formal role within the college community. Even at this early stage, she understood that this had to change, but she was not quite ready yet. At this point, the counsellor and student were addressing various and simultaneous levels of need: the need for choice, something that had been denied her when she was raped; the fact that she could have some control about how quickly to 'let the counsellor in'; her history within the family and how this had influenced her capacity to be vulnerable in the present, both in a positive and a negative way; her need for her defences to be recognized and honoured until she was ready to dismantle them. All of these provided material for the intensive next session which she reported as bringing about a change in the way she saw herself and the way she behaved with colleagues and friends.

Within one term, the waiting list for regular counselling had been dealt with and the service was able to return to normal. However, the lessons learned during that period meant that there was now a commitment to more short-term work whenever possible.

Structurally, the benefit of using the initial session in a real and therapeutic way had been recognized, or, more precisely, rediscovered. It was important also to acknowledge the inappropriateness of passing on students to another counsellor, particularly in brief work. The service therefore returned to the familiar practice of counsellors taking on students they saw in initial sessions for regular work. However, this time the parameters were different. Since the service received twenty to twenty-five requests each week for initial appointments, the counsellors agreed that for every four hours counselling they did they would have to see a new student if the waiting time were to be kept to within one week. They would then make a decision within their own timetable as to how many sessions to offer. Each counsellor was encouraged to have a small number of long-term clients, both to inform their therapeutic work and, more importantly, because that is what some students need. They were also encouraged to include some medium-term work, even if concentrating on short-term work whenever possible. However, because they were now responsible for deciding how many sessions they offered a student, a feeling of autonomy and containment re-emerged. A pilot study in 1994 to evaluate students' responses to this style of working showed that most felt that they had been given the time that they needed.

SHORT-TERM WORK

There is no doubt that increased demand has caused services to focus on the nature of short-term work. Demand-led counselling can lead to a group of frustrated counsellors being forced to offer less than their best. Though this may be the case for some, it can be argued that short-term work is, in fact, the treatment of choice in this particular setting.

There is a sense in which all work in educational institutions is about time and its limits. Students are aware that they have committed a specific amount of time in the hope of achieving a particular task. In some this may induce feelings of panic, but for others it is a motivating factor and one that can be harnessed in the therapeutic process. Mann (1973) describes how a sense of timelessness, where everything is felt to be possible, originates in the earliest stages of infancy. When an infant feels totally at one with its mother and a parallel sense of omnipotence prevails, then time is not an issue. Indeed, time does not exist. It is only with the beginning of the process of separation and individuation that time begins to be real. Mann suggests that it is this struggle between a primitive desire for timelessness and the burden of the reality of time and its finiteness that is the constant task of life and one that is always apparent in the consulting room, although often ignored. When sessions are organized so that clients/patients can re-experience that sense of timelessness with the counsellor/therapist, and yet at the same time be allowed to mourn the loss of the sense of infinite time, a more realistic knowledge of self emerges. Far from time-limited work being the poor relation of 'real' therapy, Mann sees it as creative and life-enhancing.

Students' lives are an enactment of this paradox and conflict. Their external world is governed by terms, examinations and the daily timetable; while the internal imperative is towards separation and autonomy, there is also a need to become totally absorbed, even fused, both with their subject and the experience of being a student before differentiation can begin and a capacity to be critical can be formed. If counsellors are brave enough to deal with their own wish for endless time, then they may be able to help students use its limits to advantage.

Not all students who come to counselling are in need of the kind of psychotherapeutic intervention described by Mann. ASC (1995) noted that 50 per cent of students in higher education and 70 per cent of students in further education were seen one to three times; 10 and 20 per cent respectively were seen eight times; and 3 and

5 per cent respectively were seen more than sixteen times. It can be assumed that a number of students seen one to three times presented with a specific issue that required a problem-focused approach. Some may have appeared at moments of crisis and, when their coping strategies had been mobilized, saw little use for any further work. Others may have gone away disappointed, either because the relationship with the counsellor had not been adequately formed or because they themselves did not have the capacity to sustain a continuous relationship. Some may have been referred to other more appropriate agencies. However, if as the figures show, the bulk of the work with students is generally done in under eight sessions, then the world of student counselling is challenged to find appropriate therapeutic techniques. Because the range of problems presented to these services is wide and they often have a long and complicated history, concentrating on the presenting problem alone is often not enough.

The literature on brief, psychodynamic therapy (e.g. Malan 1979) suggests that not everyone is suitable for this kind of work. This includes people in the acute stage of depression or psychosis. Some may show a faint hint of psychosis, a suggestion of a delusional element in their presentation, which, although not seriously affecting their capacity to remain in the real world (e.g. of student work), could escalate if aroused by the tension and excitement of focal work. Others who are unsuitable for short-term work include those who have a long and complicated history of loss; those who see the problem in concrete terms or as completely 'out there'; and those who deal with their anxiety by converting it into action and, in psychoanalytic terms, 'act out' their preoccupations, often in dramatic ways.

Those who can be helped by short-term counselling have some degree of psychological mindedness (i.e. they have some sense of themselves in relation to their past). They have a motivation to change and some curiosity about how things have come to be the way they are. They show some capacity to look inside themselves. The prognosis for short-term work is also good if it is clear that they have formed good relationships in the past. This is evidenced by their willingness to enter a working alliance with the counsellor. Such students need also to be able to tolerate the anxiety and frustration that short-term work inevitably gives rise to. Most importantly, there has to be in the presentation of their difficulties a focal point that can be used as the basis for the counselling work. This is something that the student and counsellor can agree upon.

Focusing on one issue in short-term dynamic counselling differs in technique from decision-making and problem-focused work in that the counsellor attempts to understand and interpret the psychodynamic elements of the focal issue. In other words, they look for evidence of where this links with personal history, of repeated patterns, and for some indication of the same issue being enacted in relation to the counsellor. As in long-term work, counsellors seek to link the past with the relationship between them and their client and with their client's response to other people or to events in the client's present everyday world. In this way, the client gains insight that brings with it the potential for change.

Ellen Noonan, in an unpublished paper, uses the analogy of the game of 'pick sticks' to underline the importance of the focal element in brief dynamic therapy. The aim of the game is to move a stick without causing movement in the surrounding and often interlinked sticks. In focal therapy, the aim is the exact opposite. It is to find the one stick that, when picked up, will create the greatest amount of movement and change in the structure.

The idea of short-term counselling within person-centred theory is almost a contradiction in terms. Person-centred counsellors believe strongly in their clients' right to self-determination, and a system that empowers counsellors to decide on the appropriate length of treatment goes against everything that is held to be central to their work. However, Brian Thorne (1994) writes of pursuing what he describes as a heretical line of thought. He wonders whether for some clients short-term counselling might be the most desirable and potentially most effective option. He goes on to describe a system of 'focused counselling' whereby clients were offered three sessions with the chance of participating in a group with others who had taken part in focused counselling but who felt there was work still to do. The students who opted for this way of working presented a variety of concerns and Thorne (1994: 63) records that in no way were their problems superficial or merely situational: 'Among them were delayed grief, the aftermath of rape, parental physical abuse, performance phobia in a performing arts student and the struggle to escape from a fundamentalist religious sect'. He continued to work with one student on an individual basis after the three sessions, but all the others were content with the work done in the scheduled time.

In examining why it was possible to work with these students in so short a time, Thorne draws some conclusions about the students' capacities for this kind of work. These conclusions parallel many of the findings of suitable characteristics within a psychodynamic framework. He summarizes:

1 these clients were all self-exploring people who intuited immediately that brief counselling would meet their needs;
2 they required a particular kind of companionship to enable
them to complete a process which was already well advanced;
3 person-centred counselling offered them that companionship
in a quintessential form.

(Thorne 1994: 63)

Thorne goes on to say that in no way were the essential ingredients
of person-centred counselling compromised. In fact, he expresses his
eagerness to repeat the experience of being able to offer acceptance,
empathy and congruence in such an intense and powerful way to
clients who have made a clear choice to engage in short-term work.

In contrast to the established criteria for successful short-term
work within psychodynamic theory, and Thorne's experience of
students who were ready and eager to work, Alex Coren (1996)
writes of short-term work with one student where the prognosis
appeared not to be good. The student was referred by his GP,
who described him as significantly depressed. He engaged in acts
of self-harm (cutting his arm with a knife). He did not want to be
in counselling and he was passive, morose and uncommunicative
in the initial consultation. He in no way was a relatively healthy,
well-functioning client who was psychologically minded and well
motivated for change.

This student was seen for three sessions over a five-week period.
During the sessions it emerged that he had moved frequently as a
child and that his father had died suddenly when the he was fourteen. (Again within the traditional diagnostic criteria, substantial
loss would have been a contraindication for brief work.) He perceived his mother as pushy and that she, and his former school, had
used their influence to secure a place for him within the university.
Although successful in his first year of study, he had consciously
avoided taking an active part in university life. He believed his
father had died from over-work at something he did not enjoy.

Coren writes of how he used the experience within the counselling room to unravel the student's inability to engage with the
counselling work and with life in the university. He was active in
the sessions and refused to collude with the student's need to keep
his dead father alive via paralysis in the sessions:

In part through my activity, Jeffrey was angry that I had disturbed his melancholy reverie, and that I was modelling or
implying an alternative way of identifying with his father which
involved being alive (or active). I attempted to link the mute

anger/passivity and frustration with anxiety (i.e. what was the nature of the anxiety being defended against?) – what would happen if Jeffrey lived? Would father or father's memory die? Was the only possible link and source of identification with his father a foreclosure of his own development?

He was annoyed with me for not colluding with this in our sessions. I wasn't going to have dead sessions. What was central, I think, was this issue of passivity/anger and its expression in three linked areas: firstly the process of the sessions (the here and now/what was going on, or not, between us, if you like); secondly, his developmental history (his family background, his dead father and what attachment to Oxford/another place might represent); thirdly his current functioning (his conscious effort to have no part in Oxford life or socialise). Since his father's death he had wanted to maintain an illusion of stasis and paralysis, in all these areas, not least his therapy. Metaphorically, in sessions, we were continuously addressing these three areas at once. For instance when we talked about the process between him and me, I was aware that we were also addressing the other two sides of his triangle, that is his past history and his current life outside the consulting room.

(Coren 1996: 28–9)

In many ways, this case illustrates the principle of brief dynamic therapy and yet it does not fit all the rules. The case, described earlier in this chapter, of the girl who was raped might more easily fit a description of crisis intervention (Caplan 1964), although there appears to be a deeper sense of change than one might expect. These two cases represent the dilemma for student counsellors as they reflect upon their work in this area. There is much that can and has been learned from other experienced practitioners and yet there are fundamental aspects which are new and, as yet, not formally evaluated. The experience of students and counsellors alike is that brief counselling works. Some counsellors are beginning to formulate an answer to why this should be so. Time to think and time to engage in sound research projects is needed to crystallize and to share these new formulations with others in the wider field of counselling, as well as to improve the delivery of effective services.

SUPERVISION

Counsellors systematically reflect upon their work during supervision. This may seem an ambiguous term to anyone outside counselling, because of the understanding of the definition of supervision within a management framework. The management of caseloads and of particular client work is an important function. When student counsellors work in teams, this is often carried out during team meetings (where cases are presented) and during regular meetings between staff members and the head of the service. Lone counsellors have to make decisions about management for themselves. However, when counsellors talk of supervision they have an explicit understanding that this takes place outside the management structure. It is a confidential relationship, usually with someone of considerably more experience, where the focus of the discussion is work with clients. Supervision takes place outside the management structure because it is recognized that working with clients produces much personal material for counsellors which may be inappropriate to discuss with colleagues and senior staff. It also allows counsellors to discuss their weaknesses and their vulnerability in the work without fear of being judged. In this way, their work with their clients is monitored and kept safe. It is also the most regular form of staff development and training in which counsellors engage. Another reason for separating management and supervision is that it allows counsellors to make clinical decisions away from the demand-led atmosphere of most services. If counsellors were to be supervised by line managers, the demands placed on the managers might affect the supervisory process by, for example, influencing a counsellor to terminate work with a client when this is not clinically appropriate.

ASC (1994) clearly stipulates in its *Requirements and Guidelines for Members Seeking Accreditation* the number of hours of supervision required:

Individual supervision for one hour should take place once a week but at least once a fortnight for counsellors with twelve or more contact hours each week.

Supervision should take place for one hour at least once a month for those counsellors with fewer than twelve contact hours each week.

Group supervision for counsellors must provide comparable access to consultative support as that for individual supervision. Counsellors with twelve or more contact hours each week should meet in a group of not more than four for a minimum of two hours per week (pro-rata for larger or smaller groups).

Counsellors with fewer than twelve contact hours each week should meet in a group of not more than four for a minimum of two hours per fortnight (pro-rata for larger or smaller groups).

These criteria are considerably more precise than those of BAC (1994) in its Accreditation Criteria, which asks for 'a minimum of one and a half hours monthly ... and a commitment to continue this for the period of accreditation'. In being so precise, ASC knows that some people find this a difficult standard to achieve. Not all institutions are convinced of the necessity of supervision. However, these criteria have been used by counsellors to negotiate with their institutions, and it is interesting to note that ASC (1995) reported that most counsellors have their supervision paid for by their institution. In further education, there was a noticeable minority where this was not the case. It is not always clear that the hours paid for by the institution meet the number required for counsellors to be eligible for accreditation or whether, in order to reach the required standard, counsellors, have to pay for additional supervision themselves.

The relationship with one's supervisor is of great importance, whether within individual, group or peer supervision. The supervisor has to be someone whom the counsellor can trust to contain anxiety, to challenge and confront and to offer new ways of looking at things. Most counsellors choose supervisors who share their theoretical orientation, although some prefer to work with supervisors whose different orientation will add a new perspective. The challenge for supervisors is to bring their own skills and understanding to the supervisory process without unduly influencing the counsellor to work in the supervisor's image. However much student counsellors may wish for a new and challenging perspective on their work, they are often faced with the dilemma of finding a supervisor who has sufficient experience of the context and practice to be of any real use. This is particularly the case when counsellors are attempting to make sense of short-term work within their supervision. It is rare to find an experienced supervisor who is committed to and enthusiastic about short-term work and this poses particular problems for student counsellors, who often find themselves having to convince their supervisors that what they are doing is of real therapeutic value.

Another subject of debate is the accountability of the supervisor to the institution in which the counsellor works. Many hold that the relationship is as confidential as that of a counsellor with a client and so refuse to report in any way to the institution unless there is any danger or risk to clients. The BAC Code of Ethics and Practice for the Supervision of Counsellors (1988) says that it is, without question, the supervisor's responsibility to report to an institution or professional body if they think a counsellor is putting

clients at risk. The assumption is that a supervisor will first negotiate with the counsellor over matters of concern, and only if this
does not produce change will they then inform the appropriate
body. However, since counsellors in educational settings state as
part of their case for the institution's payment of their supervision
that it is the single most effective way of ensuring the quality of
counsellors' work, it is not surprising that institutions sometimes
request formal feedback. Counsellors and supervisors need to be
clear about the nature of the contract and with whom it is made,
if the institution is paying for supervision. Assumptions about responsibility need to be clarified. Is the supervisor responsible first
and foremost to the client, to the counsellor or to the institution?
ASC suggests that comments from supervisors can be used at times
of inspection. The implications of this need to be taken into account
by counsellors and their supervisors when defining the nature of
their contract.

GENDER ISSUES

The roles of men and women in British society have changed greatly
recently. As many writers on the subject have developed their ideas
as members of academic communities, one might expect that these
communities would therefore be at the forefront of change. It is
questionable, however, whether this is the case.

There is no doubt that many of the changes are embodied in the
make-up of student populations. Women are attending return-to-
study courses in FE colleges; more young women in schools are
studying science subjects and making their way into universities
where, although still in the minority in most departments, they are
making their presence felt; more young men now study for nursing.
However, the atmosphere in most educational institutions is still
predominantly traditional, despite a strong commitment to policies
of equal opportunity in many establishments. Change takes time.

Tensions regarding gender issues within educational institutions
are demonstrated in differing ways. These appear in the counselling
room, as individual students attempt to make sense of their experience. Sometimes the presentation in the counselling room is of a
familiar kind: feelings of frustration with the system; a lack of clarity
about how to behave with the opposite sex in these days of changing rules. Sometimes the problem is centred on relationships with
uncomprehending partners, as mature students attempt to bring
about fundamental changes in their lives. However, other presentations, while still familiar, suggest a disturbance which is deep

within students' personal and family histories rather than a response to changing times.

Being at college or university, particularly if this requires living away from home, allows students to take themselves outside the family situation and develop a new perspective. Sometimes it is the first time they have dared to think about unspoken horrors at home. Where there has been physical, sexual or emotional abuse within the family, the secret is usually closely guarded. The college or university counselling service may present the first opportunity an individual has had to talk to someone who is not connected with statutory services and who is not under obligation to act, or who is not familiar with their own home. Sometimes it is this very distance from home that makes it possible for students to talk.

Between 1990 and 1995, student counselling services have reported a large increase nationally in the number of people needing to talk and deal with the experience of being abused. There are many students whose sense of identity as men or women in the world has been impaired as a result of the experience of being abused, whether sexually, physically or psychologically. They come and talk clearly, but with a great deal of difficulty and pain, about what they know has happened to them.

In working with such students, counsellors in further and higher education adopt approaches familiar to the counselling world in general. However, sometimes the very experience of being in education has a particular impact on the student which allows a counsellor ready access to material that would otherwise remain hidden.

A young woman came to the counselling service half way through her first-year examinations. She was finding the experience intolerable. It was not that she was afraid of the examinations *per se*. She had worked, knew her material and had never had difficulty in examinations before. To her horror, she was finding that she could not bear to be in the examination room and found that she had to force herself to stay there.

During the course of the session, the counsellor wondered with the client whether there was something about being in a room and being forced to do something to someone else's timetable. The student fell silent. After a long period sitting absolutely still and appearing to be lost completely in her own world, she looked up and began to talk slowly and painfully of her experience of being abused by her brother.

As we shall see in Chapter 4, examinations offer rich material for understanding internal struggles. Equally the need in education to be competitive, assertive, to be able to think sequentially, to make links, and to be alone with oneself in order to study, can all have an impact upon the internal world of a student, who may be preoccupied with what kind of man or woman he or she wants to be.

The immediate external world of students presents ambiguous models. Promotion for women in educational careers has always been difficult, although in further education this is being remedied more quickly than in higher education. There is now a small number of women principals in further education and an increasing number of female heads of departments, primarily within the arts and humanities. In 1994, there were three female vice-chancellors in universities; women professors are still disproportionate to the number of women in the teaching profession.

The counselling profession shows a similar pattern. It has long been seen as the province of white, middle-class females, and although there is no formal analysis of the distribution of posts according to gender within student counselling, observation of those attending ASC conferences and meetings confirms this assumption. Yet the Heads of University Counselling Services group, formed within ASC in 1991, comprises a disproportionately high number of men. This can, of course, be explained by the usual comment that women tend to be in part-time employment for a number of years and thus lose out in career terms. However, this is only part of the reason. Whether men are more acceptable to university appointing committees, or whether women are more reluctant to seek promotion, seems a fruitful area for future research. At the moment, we have anecdotal evidence only. When a young female counsellor comments upon her resignation that it is impossible to both attend to her family and to the increasing pressures of being a counsellor, we can have some understanding of her situation. Feeding on demand at work and at home is exhausting.

According to ASC (1995), 'Although the gender balance in the student population was generally not far from 50/50 overall, only a little over one third of clients, approximately, were male'. At a time when distress in the young male population in general is seen to be at its highest, and when the Samaritans report increasing numbers of male suicides in the 16–25 age group, there is clearly much work to be done to encourage young men to use counselling services. As a male undergraduate said in a counselling session, 'Even engineers have feelings, you know'.

RACE AND CULTURE

Many counsellors in Britain, particularly those in inner-city areas, have had to look carefully at their practice in order to be open to clients who are from different cultural or ethnic backgrounds. This is particularly the case in educational settings because, as education is seen to be the means to self-advancement, there is, proportionate to the general population, a high percentage of students who do not originate from the dominant culture. It has already been noted that student counsellors are predominantly white, female and middle class, and this has implications for counsellors and clients alike.

Many students come into further and higher education unclear about what is acceptable within the institution's culture. When they enter a counselling room, they may feel that there is another foreign language and another culture to master. Counsellors, for their part, may encounter individuals who do not share an understanding of the nature of personal autonomy or concepts of the 'self' and who may have an entirely different way of describing what counsellors understand to be psychological symptoms.

> A group of British student counsellors at a European conference were planning not to attend a presentation given by a Greek colleague. Her paper on the results of her research into the need for the development of autonomy in adolescents seemed to them something they knew about already. They were doubtful that they would learn anything new. When a German colleague challenged them to think about the context in which the research had been carried out (i.e. in a culture where young people live at home with their parents until they are married and where young women in particular are not encouraged to be independent), they began to see how revolutionary the research might be within such a setting. They also began to realize that their understanding of the need for autonomy was based on their cultural understanding. They went to the presentation and came away from it with fresh insights into their work with students. They had also confronted some of their own difficulties in recognizing what Wrenn (1962) has described as their 'cultural encapsulation'.

Another example of cross-cultural misunderstanding is reported by Colin Lago and Geraldine Shipton (1994), both counsellors at Sheffield University. They record the story of an African student referred to a counselling service by a GP. For weeks he had been complaining that his head itched. Various checks for the cause of this irritation revealed nothing. When a fellow doctor, who had spent some time in Africa, remembered that this was a way of describing a feeling of depression or worry, the student's needs could at last be understood.

The many nationalities that make up the educational community challenge student counsellors to examine their assumptions, their lack of knowledge and their deeply held, subjective views about the students they see. They have often to deal with young people and mature students who are straddling at least two cultures and perhaps feeling that they are understood in neither.

A young woman in an FE college was referred to the counselling service by her tutor because she had persistent migraines and seemed permanently unhappy. She revealed in the course of the first session that some months previously she had returned from her parents' home country where it had been planned that she would marry. She had known of this in advance and had not objected. However, when she met the man with whom the marriage had been arranged, she discovered him to be forty years of age, cold and disapproving of her wish to continue her education. She had been terrified and did not know what to do. She knew that she would be letting her parents down, and yet she could not face the prospect of this particular marriage. Eventually, on the eve of the wedding, she managed to talk to one of her uncles. He pointed out that she would bring disgrace on her family if she were not to go through with the wedding. He emphasized the importance of the prospective husband within the community. However, he also realized that the young woman was extremely unhappy and took the responsibility of cancelling the wedding. Since the student had returned to Britain her parents had not spoken to her. She was allowed to remain in the family home; food was delivered to her bedroom door; she was allowed to attend college but had to return home and to her room immediately; no communication between the student and her sisters was permitted.

During the course of the next few sessions, the counsellor found herself repeatedly having to confront her own feelings and assumptions about this young woman's predicament. She also realized that she had her own views about what should happen next. With great difficulty she continued trying to enter the student's world and her understanding of the issues involved. She learned to respect the student's wish to stay as much within her family's culture as possible. The student did not want to rebel, nor to leave home. She was prepared to put up with the silent treatment because she loved and respected her parents. She wished to find a way of being autonomous but not a way that would deprive her of her cultural roots.

This young woman is just one of the many students who consult counsellors in colleges and universities who are trying to reconcile their wish to live creatively in the culture of the country of their birth, while at the same time respecting the culture of their parents. Often, attending college is the first time students find themselves outside the protection of the family culture. This can bring into the open conflicts that until now had been kept under the surface for many years.

While many of these students do consult counselling services, there is concern that a number do not. ASC (1995) has shown that 67 of 152 services consulted monitor their client populations by ethnic origin. Whether this is broken down into those students who are from overseas and those who would be defined as home students is unclear. Nor is it clear from this research if the number of students from minority ethnic backgrounds using counselling services is representative of the ethnic student population as a whole. However, anecdotal evidence from most counselling services would suggest that minority ethnic students are under-represented as users of counselling services.

As part of on-going research at the University of Hertfordshire, Sara Brown notes that about 11 per cent of clients attending the counselling service come from minority ethnic groups, whereas 18 per cent of the total student population comprises students from such groups. She points out that specific stresses such as racism, discrimination and cultural dislocation can impact in a serious way on ethnic minority students and that it might be expected that vulnerability caused by these factors would lead students to use the service. In the *Counselling Service Annual Report* (1994), she postulates that black people experiencing distress are more likely to use medical services and thus follow a route down what she terms the 'heavier end of the medical model approach to psychological problems, i.e. medication, ECT and confinement in the locked wards of psychiatric hospitals'.

In an attempt to understand why minority ethnic students do not attend counselling services in the expected numbers, Brown has engaged on a series of discussions with students and lecturers who are representative of the racial and cultural groups within the university. Some of her findings suggest that students prefer to use political methods to attend to the issues of discrimination and racism. There is a strong Afro-Caribbean Society within the university, which frequently challenges the institution to consider its structures. On the other hand, students who feel uncomfortable using political means to address such issues can feel lost and alone. The concept of counselling is new and when understood at all seems to be linked in these students' minds to marriage, immigration or social welfare problems. They do not see the counselling service as a place to discuss their own personal development. In particular, some students believe that it is not possible for people from outside their culture to understand their problems and emphatically state that it is completely unacceptable within their culture to discuss problems with people from outside their families.

ASC has been very active in trying to understand how student counsellors can respond best to the specific situations of minority ethnic students. Their concern has been to make counsellors and services accessible to all students, while at the same time recognizing the need to respect cultural conventions that would see counselling as an intrusion. The association has supported the development of the RACE Division within BAC. The RACE Division has an underpinning philosophy of understanding through partnership rather than separation, and via this route ASC has increased awareness of the issues among its membership. Conferences have also been held at which issues regarding working within a culturally diverse institution have been addressed. In addition, the association has attempted to encourage services to recruit staff from minority ethnic groups.

All these methods employed by ASC and its members will take time to produce results. However, an enlightening and encouraging note was offered at the annual conference in 1994. Lennox Thomas, Director of NAFSYAT, an organization committed to counselling and psychotherapy for people from minority ethnic groups which challenges the received wisdom that such groups cannot and will not use such services, urged white counsellors to view their work with black students as essential and valuable. He spoke of the need black people feel to develop a false white persona in order to engage with the white world, which may lead them to feel cut off from their true selves. He saw the work of counsellors as helping people to regain contact with their own authenticity and suggested that the experience of being allowed to do this in the presence of a white counsellor can have a profoundly therapeutic effect for black clients.

Overseas students

During the 1970s, there was a large number of overseas students in both further and higher education. The fee policy at that time encouraged students to attend FE colleges in order to take A levels and advance to higher education. As well as gaining the necessary academic requirements for entry into higher education, students fulfilled the residency requirements while they were studying at an FE college. This entitled them to apply for a grant towards their studies at an HE institution and to be charged fees at the home student rate. By the 1980s, this facility had been removed. Overseas students were no longer able to claim residency while studying for A levels and they had to pay full cost fees at university or polytechnic. This, understandably, resulted in a drop in the number of overseas students entering higher education. In addition, the full cost was raised to a level that made it difficult for all but wealthy students to apply. This change in status was the subject of great controversy. Nevertheless, many institutions set up highly sophisticated international offices, whose task was to recruit as many overseas students as possible. Occasionally, they included in their team international student advisers to attend to the after-sales service, some of whom had counselling training, but most of whom did not.

The term 'overseas students' tells us something about the ambivalence in the relationship between the institution and these students. It is at one and the same time welcoming and distancing. It is a euphemism for 'foreign', but the word 'overseas' leaves such students in no doubt that they are perceived as being oceans apart from their new institution. This ambiguity in the relationship becomes very apparent to students early during their stay in Britain and can bring them to the counselling service in a state of shock and then anger.

On the whole, universities and colleges of higher and further education seem not to be aware of the impact that the transition to a new educational institution and a new country has on their students. Although induction courses are often offered, once completed the students are expected to make their own transition and to behave and study as if they were fully assimilated into the dominant culture.

Lago and Shipton (1994), in writing about 'international students', describe four stages of culture shock. In the first stage, the student enjoys a honeymoon period when everything is new and exciting. However, during this period, which may last some time, they may also experience difficulties in communication, a sense of loss and isolation. This feeling of disorientation, which can be accompanied by increasing apathy, leads the student into the second stage of transition, which Lago and Shipton call 'disintegration'. At this point, the student may become quite depressed and many have strong wishes to withdraw from the course.

During the third stage of 'reintegration', the student begins to rediscover the value of their own differences. But in doing so, they may become angry, suspicious and rebellious. At this point they may become highly critical of the host culture. Holding on to an understanding of the psychological implications of culture transition seems doubly important for the counsellor at this time. The temptation might be to collude with the student's criticisms, particularly if the counsellor knows, as suggested earlier, that there is a strong element of truth in what the student is saying. Knowing that there are internal and significant personal reasons for students to come to their own point of resolution may help the counsellor to avoid adding to the student's sense of outrage and injustice.

Lago and Shipton's comments on the final stages of development, 'autonomy' and 'independence', are hopeful yet salutary:

> Self-assurance, a renewed sense of independence and a capacity to become expressive and creative typify these fourth and fifth stages. In the fifth stage the person has achieved what is called 'bi-cultural competence', a capacity to feel competent and at home in both cultures. This is a very sophisticated stage to achieve and there is no guarantee that everyone will reach it.
>
> (Lago and Shipton 1994: 54)

One of the ways in which student counsellors deal with their own anger at how overseas students and British-born but culturally different students are treated, is to feed their perceptions back to the institution in a productive way. Thus a number of counsellors have been involved in developing staff development programmes. Colin Lago has been actively involved in working in this way for a number of years and at one point was allowed sabbatical leave to write up the content of his training programmes (Lago 1990). His work and his personal commitment have been an important resource for members of both ASC and BAC, as well as for his own university. However, it is interesting to note that when he presented an overview of the potential for training academic colleagues in this area at a conference of European student counsellors, his ideas met with considerable resistance from some. At best, a number felt that the culture in their own organizations would not allow them to work in this way; at worst, others could not see how this work should in any way be part of the role of a counsellor. Another cultural gap had emerged and the conference organizers (a cross-national group) were astonished at the reaction Lago's presentation had provoked.

Some of the feelings aroused in counsellors on behalf of students from other cultures have their basis in reality. It is clear that these students are often subjected to a lack of understanding, racism and injustice. Those who are culturally different become easy targets for projection. To deal with this issue, counsellors have tried to make themselves more informed, recognizing that a fear of the unknown can be turned into a fear of the unknown person; they have attended workshops where they have attempted to confront some of their assumptions and prejudices; they have learned to ask their clients about aspects of the clients' world they have found foreign; they have begun to look at how psychological problems are expressed and treated within other cultures. However, many student counsellors find that the best way of approaching this issue is via a systematic study of their work with such students through supervision and personal reflection. In doing this, they allow the students to become the teachers.

In an unpublished paper, Craig McDevitt (1994) of Edinburgh University illustrates the need for counsellors to monitor their own internal world. He describes his work with a German student who initially made him feel small and ridiculous. The student had begun by interviewing McDevitt about his credentials:

> He wanted to know my qualifications, my length of experience, my theoretical orientation, my philosophy of life and with each answer I gave, his face remained impassive, revealing nothing of his reactions. This and a sensation of being pushed into a position of passivity, gave rise to me of feelings of anxiety and defensiveness. During this 'interview' I was thinking that his need to check my credentials was possibly a defence, his formal interviewing manner, against an anxiety that it was unsafe to be here but I also felt reluctant to make this interpretation to him because it felt like an appalling breach of social etiquette to mention personal emotions, especially fear,

in the formal context he had created. I also felt that to touch on his feelings would offend and consequently alienate him. Nevertheless, I started to formulate a feeling response in my mind with the awareness that if I did not begin to interact with him, if I did not resist my own passivity in the face of his cold teutonic correctness (as I was seeing his behaviour in my own mind), I would become alienated and so would he.

It is important to note that McDevitt had chosen to write about a German student because he had studied in Germany, worked and developed relationships there and felt an affection for the country and the people he had met there. In many ways, it was not a foreign culture but one where he felt at home. However, he also acknowledged the violent history shared by Scots and Germans and, coming from the immediate post-war generation, the ambivalent and confusing feelings that could be generated in him in threatening situations with Germans.

McDevitt's paper gives a full account of the student's problems and his understanding of them within the student's history. However, it is the commentary within the paper on his own feelings that provides insight into how counsellors use counter-transference to understand the internal culture of students and to monitor those aspects within themselves that might interfere with the therapeutic process. At the end of the session he records:

He shook my hand again as he left but this time the grip was not so hard and I wondered if what I had felt with the previous handshake was less an aggressive act but more of a desperate need to hold onto someone or something.

On reviewing the session I was struck by how much he had made me feel small, inadequate and foolish especially when he laughed at my suggestion to take 'ridiculous' things seriously. I felt it possible this was how he himself felt. I was also pleased with myself for not taking on the authority role, the expert, but to leave it very firmly in his hands. The temptation for me in the face of his behaviour was to take on authority as a way of defending myself against the anxiety that I was inadequate. I knew that I had seen him as some stereotypical German, efficient and domineering but he did tell me that his family were more German than the Germans and this raised in my mind that the family were trying to live out a stereotypical and unrealistic image of what it meant to be truly German. All in all, I was aware that I did not know who Wolfgang really was and I strongly suspected that Wolfgang did not really know himself. I found this quite confusing and consequently had the urge to pick up the 'phone and ask a German colleague to try and explain this client to me, to tell me about the culture he came from, to tell me how much he deviated from the norm of German youth but I rejected the idea although I knew that it might help me to cut corners. I rejected it because I felt I had already made a commitment to Wolfgang that he would be the expert, that it would be he who told me about him.

This case illustrates the importance of confronting personal prejudices and assumptions, however painful or embarrassing that might be, in order to hear what the client is saying. A failure to do this would have resulted in a rejection of the student and a rejection of the counsellor's own feelings, thus reducing the capacity to understand them and their origin. In understanding them more clearly, it was possible to discern which of the student's difficulties were cultural and which were familial in origin.

All counsellors have the opportunity to work with people from other cultures, but the concentration of minority ethnic and overseas students in education has allowed student counsellors to develop skills and understanding that are of benefit to the profession as a whole. This is true of other issues which are specific to student counselling but which are significant to generic counsellors, especially those who are interested in adolescent development or who are working with individuals who inevitably revisit that stage of their development through the process of further or higher education. It is these specific issues that are addressed in the next chapter.

· FOUR ·

Specific issues in student counselling

Working with students is exciting. They are people who usually start from the position that change is possible. If counsellors can harness this impetus, then they have an opportunity of working with a potent, forward-moving dynamic. Compared with those whose primary area of work is with the recently unemployed, the terminally ill or the bereaved, student counsellors are very fortunate in their client group and their educational setting.

There is a particular excitement when working with articulate people who can use symbols and metaphor. This can give access to rich and varied material.

A mature student whose specialism was medieval history
had been struggling with serious life events that had stirred
up earlier feelings of abandonment by a stern and
uncompromising mother. She found her confused feelings
unmanageable and was distressed that she seemed incapable
of finding some form within her inner chaos.

During one session she recounted a trip to a cathedral
where the spire was being restored. Two women, who were
senior members of the restoration team, had taken her up
in a lift to view the work in progress. She was able to look
inside the spire. What had amazed her was the lack of
obvious regular form. 'It was a mess', she said, 'Nothing
seemed to fit. And yet there it was . . . this mess of bits and
pieces that together forms something beautiful that has been
there for hundreds of years'. She went on to talk of how
she would have liked to think that her mind was akin to a
geodesic dome, beautifully symmetrical and perfectly

designed. But now she could see that however chaotic it might really be, there was the possibility of restoring something of substance.

The woman counsellor hardly needed to comment on the significance of the fact that the two of them had trusted each other enough to take the student to potentially dangerous heights in order to look inside herself. The student had all but made the link on her own.

It would be foolish to suggest that all students are equally intellectually gifted or psychologically minded, but there are many who are and who can use the counselling relationship to give them new and unexpected insights. Often, counsellors as a professional group are suspicious of intelligence, seeing in it the possibility of intellectualization as a means of defence against uncomfortable material. Intellectualization is certainly a hazard for those who counsel students. But not all students are extraordinarily intelligent; neither are they more than normally psychologically defended. They may, however, adopt this additional way of expressing their defensiveness.

A broad range of understanding is needed in student counselling, because of the varied backgrounds and experiences students bring with them to college. Some have great difficulty with academic work; others have a facility with words and concepts that is greater than the counsellor's. A single university or college may have a population of up to 15,000 full-time students. In 1994, a post advertising for a new head of the joint counselling service for Manchester University, the University of Manchester Institute of Science of Technology and the Royal Northern College of Music indicated a constituent population of 23,100. Offering a counselling service to what is, in effect, the equivalent of a large town, requires that the counsellors are able to respond to a variety of demands. The problems presented will be as wide as the population it serves. Student counsellors therefore need to be skilled in assessment procedures, to be experienced in much more than a single problem area, and to have considerable flexibility in their practice. However, there are issues which have a specific relevance to this setting and which experienced student counsellors recognize as central to their work.

THE SIGNIFICANCE OF THE ACADEMIC YEAR
AND ITS DEMANDS

The academic year and the round of tasks to be undertaken are an ever-present reality for academics and students alike. They may also have a symbolic significance for a number of students, but the reality of the structure itself cannot be denied.

Students have to learn to manage their time and their resources, both those outside and around them, and those inside them which are at times elusive, and they have to manage their relationship with the institution and its demands. If they are unable to do this, they are failing in their task of being a student. They bring these realities to counselling, and counsellors have to decide whether or not to ally themselves with the learning task. At times this involves recognizing that such demands are more pressing than the completion of a full piece of therapeutic work. Missed sessions because a class has been changed may be the reality of academic life. It does not necessarily mean a resistance to counselling. Pressure to produce work on time or to perform well in examinations is not always due to the pressure of internal persecutory figures. This is the student's real world.

Some counsellors, new to the educational setting, find these aspects an intrusion. It takes time for them to realize that the completion of these external tasks can, in itself, be therapeutic. Particularly for adolescents who strive towards autonomy, the steps towards completing a course may also signify strides in the process of becoming independent. Experienced student counsellors do not ignore or become frustrated by these demands of time, the necessity to perform and the rigours of assessment processes. Instead, they work with them as real issues, as well as helping students to understand their deeper, unconscious, significance.

Beginnings

When students begin college or university, they have to find their place in an institution that is larger and more complex than any they have known previously. The process of negotiating the first few days and weeks can be daunting. Sadly, some never achieve this sense of knowing where they are and what they are there to do.

Whether a student is young or old, extremely clever or not so clever, articulate or lost for words, the issues at the beginning are the same. Students need to leave behind what has gone before and to look forward to what is to come. They need to become attached to the institution and to their subject, to make friends and to form a working relationship with those who will teach them. For those leaving home for the first time, there are the additional tasks of finding somewhere to live and looking after themselves. Many students have, for the first time, to manage their own finances, to balance basic needs and have a social life with the costs of accommodation, books and equipment.

Many colleges and universities run a formal induction course which attempts to recognize the many and often conflicting demands, and to orientate students to the institution and to their course. Counsellors are often involved in these programmes, either by giving brief, introductory talks explaining the service and how to find it, or conducting sessions where students are encouraged to talk to each other about the process of settling in, for example.

With all these issues to be dealt with, it is not surprising that counselling services are used generally by more people in their first year than at any other time.

Academic terms

In further education, the academic terms are usually fourteen weeks long, in new universities twelve weeks, old universities ten weeks, and Oxford and Cambridge universities eight weeks. This means that in every beginning there is an end in sight and this has impact on the students' approach to their academic work and to their counselling.

For young people living away from home, this time-limited independence can be both positive and negative. On the positive side, it allows them to try out independence knowing that there is somewhere to go back to, even if, ostensibly, it is only to deal literally or metaphorically with their dirty washing. On the negative side, there is a constant shift from developing adulthood to being a child in the family home. One university student remarked that it takes four weeks to settle in each term, two weeks to work and four weeks to prepare to leave again. If this is true, then those with eight-week terms have a problem!

For those who cannot go home, either for reasons of geographical or emotional distance, there is an added dynamic. Their sense of being different is underlined. Problems of extreme loneliness during vacation periods often arise. Counselling services tend to remain open for most, if not all, of vacation periods. This is partly because they recognize that for some regular clients problems do not fit neatly into the framework of terms, but also because an increasing number of students stay in the area of the university or college because they have already paid for their accommodation. Some mature students also live locally and graduate students do not work within the format of terms.

When students come for counselling shortly before term ends, counsellors always asks the question (even if only of themselves), 'Why now?' Counsellors listen carefully for the following reasons, particularly if they are unrecognized by the student: some students panic just before term ends because of the work they have not done; some cannot bear the thought of going home; others leave counselling to the last minute in the hope that nothing too distressing will be stirred up; others have unrealistic ideas of what can be achieved in one or two sessions. On the positive side, some students make a conscious decision that, with less academic work to do, they can concentrate on the emotional side of their development for a while. Such a sense of timing is healthy and can motivate them to work as hard in the counselling sessions as they have done in term on their academic work. Although some counsellors might see this as an unhealthy split between the academic and the personal self, others would understand this as a sign that the student is in touch with what can, and cannot, be managed concurrently.

The middle period

When the initial excitement and anxiety of joining the institution is over and the rhythm of terms mastered, students begin a different stage. They now have to be consistent and persistent and sustain their curiosity, and the meaning of the course to them and their future lives becomes a predominant theme. Some face this question very early when they discover that they have made the wrong choice and either leave or try to change courses. Even students who have few doubts about the appropriateness of their studies at this time might question why they are there and what they are doing.

There is a time in all academic work when students become discouraged. Learning means taking on new ideas and having to lose some that are old, and this creates uncertainty.

A mature student who had been a policeman found himself disturbed by aspects of his social science course. He had always regarded himself as liberal in his views, but now he felt his sense of identity was challenged by what he was learning. He had joined the course because he wanted to change. At the point of change he did not know what he might become.

Even when the content of an academic course is not as obviously relevant to personal development as it was for this student, any learning can at some point produce a feeling of being deskilled. It is a normal and natural process in education to recognize how little you know and how much more there is to learn. It is usually at this point that students are forced to ask themselves what they want to achieve and why they want to achieve it. Many students negotiate this difficult period successfully and their curve of motivation begins to climb again, but in a realistic and steady way.

When a student comes for counselling during this period of their academic career, the counsellor might not just ask why the student is doing the course but for whom. Too often their choice of subject has been made to satisfy others. Sometimes this is the result of a conscious feeling of pressure or, more benignly, as a result of suggestion: 'You're good at maths and making things. What about a course in engineering?' Sometimes the reason for pursuing a course is more subtle and more difficult to fathom: an unconscious desire to appease parental figures or a need to gratify an unexplored aspect of the self. Whether the reason is conscious or unconscious, students need help to understand if they are to be able to make a real and informed choice about continuing with their studies.

Endings

While each end of term is a rehearsal for the ending of a course of studies, nothing can prepare students enough for the powerful effects of leaving university or college and moving on into the outside world. As with all mourning processes, the experience of letting go is governed by the quality of the immediate relationship, as well as by the way loss has been dealt with in the past. For those for whom this is an end to formal education, there can be many mixed feelings: relief, regret about things not achieved, excitement and fear about what lies ahead, and the recognition that this is a turning point. For young people in particular, there is often a feeling, even if not articulated, that they must now become adults. For mature students, there is a sense that they have committed themselves to becoming a different kind of adult. All students, in one way or another, have to say goodbye to a self that they have known for many years.

The ending process in education is further complicated by the fact that it usually coincides with examinations. Being examined is such an important issue that it requires a section to itself. However, one of the significant features about examinations is the way in which people retreat into themselves. Students begin to feel that they are losing one another before they actually leave, or they discover that their friends and colleagues are changing before their very eyes. A student who had taken a year out in the middle of her course was thankful that she had had the experience of seeing her former contemporary colleagues taking their final examinations a year before her. She felt more prepared for the change that would take place in people whom she thought she knew well. She linked it with the process of ending, saying that had she not seen this in advance, she would have most likely ended the course feeling very discouraged and lost, and doubting her capacity to make judgements about people. 'The awful thing is', she said, 'they turn into creatures that you really don't like. It would have been dreadful to have left thinking that they were like that all along'.

At the same time as they are dealing with all this, students have to look ahead. They are supposed to find a job or secure a place on another course. Since what happens in the future is probably dependent on examination results, this is a time of great uncertainty. They find themselves looking backwards and looking forwards at the same time, just as they did at the beginning of the course, but this time the tension may be unbearable. It is not surprising that some lose their equilibrium. Some students retreat into the past, over-idealizing their course and experiencing their loss of friends as the end of the world. It seems impossible to think of a future life. Other students deny the end by convincing themselves that they will not miss anyone, least of all their lecturers, and that their life ahead will be the most exciting yet.

Students are well known for boisterous rites of passage to celebrate the end of examinations and courses. They are unconsciously recognizing the need to mark the end of one phase of their lives so that they can move on to the next. While the exuberance in these celebrations suggests to the outsider total relief that everything is over, those who work with students know that there is ambiguity in such seemingly manic behaviour. For some students this is a time of great risk, and the tension is simply intolerable.

Although it is enriching to work with the excitement that young people experience in education, and with people who are basically healthy and fundamentally optimistic, student counselling is no less arduous than other forms of counselling. Some counsellors may want to become student counsellors to remind themselves of the positive side of their own university or college experience and at a deeper level may still hold the view that school, college or university represents the 'best days of your life'. An idealized view of educational life serves neither the counsellor nor their students well, for they have not thought about the immense misery and

distress among the student population. Others choose student counselling because they need to recapitulate what, for them, has been
a difficult experience. At best, these motives, when worked through,
make the counsellor more aware of and sympathetic to the student's plight. At worst, the counsellor begins to identify with the
student who sees educational establishments as full of persecutory
figures who care for no-one. Student counselling provides counsellors, if they are not careful, with their own opportunity to be perpetual students.

GRADUATE STUDENTS

Although graduate study is seen as the pinnacle of achievement, it
can be one of the poor relations in the educational system. Many
find real pleasure in further study, making an important contribution to scholarship or research. But it is a competitive and often
lonely pursuit, with no guarantee of reward at the end. In Chapter
2, we saw how difficult it is to find funding and how the prospects
for employment may not improve with additional qualifications.
Here we look at some of the psychological imperatives that may be
contained in the desire for further study.

For some there really is a need to be a perpetual student. By
choosing not to leave education, they are foreclosing on an important developmental phase. Some students are almost conscious of
this and say quite openly that they do not yet feel ready to find a
job. By this they mean that they are not ready to become an adult.
These students may be aware of their need to develop further psychologically and may be seen as making a healthy decision to use
the resources available to them to try to achieve that task. The
problem arises when students do not recognize that this is why they
have chosen to continue with their studies. Frequently, they present
at counselling services with an inability to write up their work.
They have enjoyed their research, but they cannot finish. They may
have advanced academically, but they are still at the same stage
psychologically as when they began.

Graduate students frequently present at the counselling service
because they have become isolated and lost in their work. There are
identifiable external reasons, since most graduates have to work on
their own. This is what graduate studies are about and what can
bring delight to many. However it can be a hazardous occupation
for those who have a compelling need to find the answer to an
imponderable question. They use their research as a means of delving

deeper and deeper in a seemingly desperate attempt to find the elusive truth. When they come to counselling they are profoundly lost and it can take a long time before the unspoken question, which has provoked this desperate search, can be uncovered.

Potentially, the most difficult aspect of being a graduate student concerns the relationship with one's supervisor. Supervisors have considerable power over what students should research. Sometimes students are allocated a place in the department to carry out specific research, within a project headed by the supervisor, for which funding has been sought for the team as a whole. This is often the case in scientific research. The benefit to students is that they have a structure within which to work and a team with whom they meet, even if not on a regular basis. The disadvantage for some is that the agenda is set entirely by the supervisor. It is not unusual to find students coming to counselling to work out how to handle a supervisor whom they feel is rigid and closed to new ideas. Other students have to find their own topic for research and have a less specific relationship with their supervisor. While they may enjoy the freedom to pursue their own line of thinking, they can suffer from such an attenuated relationship that they can feel that they have no supervisor at all.

These are just two examples from either ends of the spectrum of relationships between supervisors and students, but they illustrate a central theme. Unless they have been undergraduates at one of the few universities that still operate a one-to-one, or one-to-two, tutorial system, postgraduates find themselves returning to what can be an intense relationship with a specific figure of authority. The power balance in this relationship is real, but it can also re-awaken past, unresolved issues about dependency, authority and rivalry. So a graduate student who complains in counselling about a supervisor who is never there and who does not care, or another who talks in fury of a rigid and demanding supervisor may be expressing something about an earlier, important relationship that originally caused them equal pain. This can be a powerful problem for graduate students who, in a very real sense, are almost totally dependent on the approval of their supervisors. For those who are engaged on research of an individual nature, there are often no others around to deflect what feels like the gaze of the parent. For those working in teams, there can be a heightened sense of rivalry as if they are brothers and sisters vying for a parent's attention.

Graduate students may be fewer in number than undergraduates but they are big users of counselling services. Since they are also older, their problems are often more entrenched and require longer-term work. At Oxford and Cambridge, long-term therapeutic groups have been established for graduates which addresses their sense of isolation. At the same time, they offer an opportunity for in-depth work on developmental issues to be addressed.

MATURE STUDENTS

In many ways, mature students share similar issues with graduate students. They also experience the resurgence of feelings of dependency at a time when they expect to be independent and may be shocked at the power of these feelings. Mature students make great demands on course tutors and are often the generators of change in teaching methods. They bring experience and a sense of commitment to the course and can be among the most successful students. Just as they have high expectations of the course and of their teachers, they expect a great deal from themselves. They can be extremely frustrated and discouraged if they do not achieve their own high standards.

When mature students give up a job to re-enter education, or if they have been unemployed for some time, it is easy to understand why success is so important to them, but other difficulties can arise if their reasons for being at university or college have hidden significance.

In some ways, all mature students are attempting to correct a part of their life that feels, however unconsciously, to have been unsatisfactory. Some are aware of the opportunity they missed previously for entry into further or higher education. Others see the choices they made in their teenage years to be no longer satisfying. Often they come into education with an expressed need for personal development, including sometimes a conscious or unconscious desire to change their relationship with close family members. A frequent problem presented in counselling is when mature students know that they are changing but are frustrated by partners or children who apparently want them to remain as they are. It is often the case that a student's own ambivalence about change, and the possibility of moving away from important people in the family, has to be explored.

Just like graduate students, mature students may be searching for an answer in their studies to something which cannot be achieved by study alone. It is to the credit of mature students that many of them negotiate this period of challenge and change with great determination and emerge at the end of their studies much closer to the person they had hoped to become.

STUDY AND STUDY SKILLS

Student counsellors need to understand the external demands on students, and then explore what such demands might mean for individuals. Frequently, students begin their first counselling session with the words, 'I've come here because I can't study'. This is perhaps to be expected given the context. Students sometimes put up with a number of worries as long as they are able to work. If their work starts to suffer, it is then they recognize the seriousness of these concerns. On the other hand, for some students, the first sign that anything is wrong is the disruption of their studies. They come to counselling anxious and puzzled about why they are failing at the very thing they came to college or university to do.

Just as counsellors check out the reality of the physical symptoms people describe when seeking counselling, so student counsellors check out perceived difficulties with studying: Are the difficulties new or is there a history to them? Do they happen continuously or only at certain times? Has the student consulted his or her tutor? Is their difficulty completely incapacitating or just a nagging worry? If the counsellor concludes that this is a suitable area for counselling, rather than for referral to other agencies, then the method employed may well be governed by the time of year the student appears, as well as by the counsellor's preferred theoretical model. A psychodynamically trained counsellor, who is more used to looking for the symbolic meaning in the study difficulty, may recognize that such an approach is not appropriate for all students, particularly if they appear just before examinations. A more behavioural or cognitive approach might then be called for. The number of specifically trained cognitive or behavioural counsellors in student counselling is small, but the influence of these theories in the area of study difficulties is great. There are no national figures available of how many use these methods, but conversations with student counsellors indicate that a large number have supplemented their main training, either by learning from experienced practitioners or by attending short courses, and that they are happy to switch methods if it is necessary. Some are less comfortable with the need to change approach, but are pragmatic enough to use other techniques if they are helpful. It is worth considering how different theoretical models may be employed in dealing with study problems.

Behavioural/cognitive approach

Underlying this method is the assumption that behaviour has been learned and can be unlearned, and that patterns of thinking can be altered. When students come to counsellors who work in this way, the focus is what needs to be changed and appropriate strategies for achieving this.

Many people, including students, have problems with procrastination: they know a piece of work has to be done, have a clear idea of what will happen if they do not complete the work, yet still cannot make themselves do it. One of the first things that a behavioural counsellor might do is to ask the student to keep a diary of how their time is spent. This gives a basis from which to work together. The next stage might then be to compile a realistic timetable allowing space for leisure and social activities as well as the more mundane tasks of eating, sleeping and carrying out domestic chores. This begins to address the frequently held idea that there is not enough time to do everything, and the secondary belief that since it is impossible to do everything, then there is no point in starting anything. Students are surprised to discover that they can structure their time as if they were in paid employment, using the framework of a working week with a fixed number of hours. This also begins to create a visible structure that provides some students with the key. They come into education from school or employment where each hour has been timetabled and the unstructured nature of student life has left them without a focus.

Within such a timetable, students might be asked to address how study time is managed. How do they set about reading? Do they read aimlessly or so as to answer specific questions? Do they know how to use the index in a book or how to scan chapters for relevant detail or summaries? Counsellors may begin to look at methods for taking notes and whether this is the most efficient way forward for a particular student. There is also the matter of retrieval of information. Not surprisingly, some students find that the task of bringing order to their random thoughts can be overwhelming at first. It is also important that each student finds a place for study that is right for them.

Counsellors can also provide information on research on learning theory, or draw from their own experience of a particular subject in their specific institution, giving information about what a student can reasonably be expected to do. Sometimes students are enormously relieved when they are told that it is perfectly legitimate to study for short periods of time, and that long periods of study without breaks impair their capacity for recall. They may have been unable to get down to work because the thought of locking themselves away for many hours was so daunting. Permission to take breaks and to have fun in these breaks can liberate them from an incapacitating sense of obligation.

More complicated areas might also be looked at: the student's sense of self-esteem and where this originates; motivation to succeed and what might interfere with it; whether a student is capable of sustaining activity to achieve long-term goals or whether shorter-term goals need to be set. Counsellors may also look at whether the course is too challenging or not challenging enough; whether there is a need to respond to authority figures by being rebellious; whether there is lack of positive feedback; or whether the problems are an early response to examination anxiety.

Throughout all this, the aim is to help students to analyse their own thoughts and responses and to plan and implement change. Exercises and homework are often set between sessions, used both for self-monitoring and for the counsellor to offer reinforcement when there is positive change.

Counsellors who also use a cognitive approach try to help students identify the beliefs that lie behind their behaviour. What are the hidden assumptions that might interfere with their capacity to study? A simple example is students who say that they cannot study because they do not like being apart from their friends. Behind this might be the belief that if they lose immediate contact with their friends, this will lead to their friends not wanting to see them. The equation has been made; the consequence of study is no friends. Identifying false beliefs and the feelings attached to them and then working on ways to challenge such beliefs forms one focus of the cognitive approach.

Behavioural and cognitive counsellors tend to be active and directive in sessions and put their expertise at the disposal of their clients where appropriate. This approach can be of great value to students who want to see more immediate evidence of change in their behaviour, thoughts and actions.

Person-centred approach

Person-centred counsellors work from the premise that it is the quality of the relationship itself that is therapeutic. They also believe that students have the capacity within themselves to bring about change if the conditions are right. Their aim in the sessions is to create those conditions.

Person-centred counsellors do not ignore the need for practical information and advice, but they have their own views as to where and how this should be presented. A good example of this can be found in the practice of David Acres, who for fourteen years was a counsellor at what was Plymouth Polytechnic. Since 1993, he has been responsible for the Learning Support Unit at the College of St Mark and St John in Plymouth. He has written and broadcast widely on study and study skills and his book, *How to Pass Exams Without Anxiety* (Acres 1994b), contains advice on how to manage course work, revision techniques, working with colleagues, examination preparation and coping with anxiety. Many of his ideas are recognizable to behavioural counsellors.

Where he differs from behavioural counsellors is in the use he makes of this material. He has built up a resource centre that students can use, which contains pamphlets, audio- and videotapes, books and, perhaps even more importantly, a collection of students' own ideas on what has worked for them in specific circumstances. His role is to be alongside students as they explore and discover what is appropriate for them. From time to time he is active, but he constantly questions who will benefit most from such interventions. His preferred role, and the one that he deems to be most effective, is that of 'assistant' and 'companion' to students. His philosophy and method is encapsulated in the following statement:

> If I feel I am 'working hard' it is probably a sign that something less than helpful or therapeutic is happening; often when I am feeling most useful to my client, I appear to be doing very little and that feels right to both me and them.
>
> (Acres 1994a:2)

This nurturing relationship with a counsellor is a fundamental experience for many students who feel lost and cut off from increasingly busy teachers, or who have little or no sense of an internal parent who cares for and nourishes them. If they can use this relationship, their capacity to trust themselves, their resourcefulness and their ability to study will improve.

Psychodynamic approach

Psychodynamic counsellors also take note of external circumstances, students' capacity to make use of practical information and resources, and the quality of the counselling relationship. But they also look for evidence as to how the counselling relationship might parallel the student's relationship to study. They attempt to discover what the study difficulty *represents* for the student.

A male student, who was following a course in travel and tourism, came to see the counsellor because, among other things, he was having great difficulty with his economics course. He had passed his GCSEs with high grades in all subjects, including mathematics, and could not understand why he should now be faced with this difficulty. His manner was very friendly, perhaps a shade too friendly, and he seemed very eager to please the female counsellor.

He travelled ninety miles to college each day by train and was resentful that this long journey restricted his social life within college. He said this would not have been the case had he not had to move to his present home just before college started. His father, who was a bank manager, was moved to another branch. There was no chance of him receiving a grant which might have allowed him to pay for accommodation nearer to college.

He described how he and his mother were at war with his father over the size of the telephone bill as each attempted to stay in contact with friends from their former home. He painted a picture of a family that had been full of resentment for many years, where the difficulties had become focused on the consequences of the forced move.

The counsellor was interested in the student's wish to keep in contact with old friends. He seemed to think that the only possibility was by telephone. The journey to see friends would be too complicated and could never be done. (In fact, it was less than a half-hour travelling distance from college.) The counsellor thought this very curious in someone who hoped for a career in travel and tourism.

When she asked him – as she often did with students who were facing study difficulties – to describe to her what economics was about, he said: 'It's about money and the power of money'. He said this with such force that the meaning was clear. The counsellor used the evidence of the session, the quality of his attempt at a collusive relationship with her, the description of him and his mother united against the bank manager father for a number of years, and the power of his description of the meaning of economics, to help her understand why the student should be having difficulty with his subject.

It is not always so easy to see the symbolism in the material presented. Even when it is clear, the student may not be ready to hear. If interpretations are shared with a student too early, then they can be dismissed as rubbish. When the timing is right, an interpretation can make sense and alter the way students view their work.

Many student counsellors, regardless of their theoretical orientation, accept the importance of working in the area of study and study skills. This is a major contribution they can make to the educational process. Some of the work is done in preventative sessions, in anxiety management workshops, in groups as well as with individuals, and through training and seminar presentations to teaching colleagues. While there is no doubt that there is value in more preventative and developmental work, doubts are raised in both counsellors' and tutors' minds as to how far this should be the province of counsellors. Chapter 6 addresses some of these issues.

CHOICE OF SUBJECT

It has been suggested that some actors take to the stage because they are shy and often lost for words. Similarly, students may choose a course of study to compensate for some personal difficulty or dissatisfaction. Such a choice may be made consciously. However, problems may arise when there are unconscious aspects to the choice of course and the student comes to the counselling service because something seems to be going seriously wrong.

A female PhD student came to the counselling service because she was depressed. Her parents, who were both academics, were philosophers of the logical positivist school. They believed that there was no value in emotions. As a child she had been taught that everything could be debated to logical conclusions and she had tried to carry this principle into her adult life.

Her research was the work of the philosopher Thomas Hobbes. She was trying to show that his work had been influenced by his time, that his ideas had grown out of a period full of Elizabethan conceit (i.e. the emotional side of life); and that the poetry, the music and the drama of this great period of English literature could be seen in his writings.

Despite her fascination with the subject and her conscious wish to complete her research, her feelings of deep depression were interfering with her capacity to work. When she was shown how closely her academic work mirrored her internal struggles to give value to feelings she was startled, amused and relieved. She was then able to talk more openly about her turbulent early childhood and adolescence and she began to understand how her depression might be linked to feelings (until then unnamed and unvalued) that had persisted into her adult life.

Counsellors work with the material presented by a client, and know that nothing expressed in a counselling session is coincidental. In further and higher education, counsellors have learned to understand the significance of the setting, the subject chosen and a student's relationship to study in particular ways. This also prepares them to deal with the specific problems which arise at the time of examinations.

EXAMINATIONS

Examination anxiety occurs not only immediately before examinations, for it is discernible throughout the entire academic year, even at its very beginning. Anxiety about examinations can permeate the whole system of education and the careers of individual students. We can understand the anxiety about this testing time: it is the culmination of students' and lecturers' work. Some students feel that it is not just their academic progress that is being evaluated, but their very selves; they equate a high pass grade with being a high grade person. Where there is continuous assessment, the focus on the end of year may not be so great, but then there is a *continuous* level of anxiety about evaluation.

Some students, of course, love examinations. Their adrenalin increases, they become more motivated and they relish the opportunity to show what they have learned. At the end of their examinations, they feel that something important has been completed; their goal has been achieved. Most students negotiate the vagaries of examination systems without needing to consult a counsellor. However, in those who do, student counsellors can discern common themes.

Large examination halls can make some students feel that they have lost their sense of identity; they become a number on a page.

A student who was taking A levels for the first time
described how he even spelt his name incorrectly. He could
not remember who he was. After some sessions of
counselling he was able to resit the examinations, and go on
to higher education where he was able to demonstrate his
considerable academic ability.

For some students, examinations mean that they have to produce
something perfect that can be admired in public. If this is linked
unconsciously with earlier public incidents where they have felt
shame, then examinations become arenas of exposure and success
seems impossible.

One student was helped through her counselling to see the
links between her fear of examinations and her sense of
guilt about having terminated a pregnancy a few years
earlier. It was as if she believed that she would never be
able to produce anything good again, while at the same
time she desperately needed to produce something that was
perfect. She was in danger of aborting her chance of success.

Examinations require students to be in touch with healthy, competitive and aggressive drives, and for many this lends an air of enjoyable excitement to the process. This may also lead to considerable
dishonesty among friends and colleagues (e.g. about the amount
of time and effort put into revision). The natural tendency to compare oneself with others can prove to be very difficult when it
comes to examinations, as students see others who spend every
available hour in the library and others who seem to do no work
at all. Such competitive feelings can get in the way of success. Some
students have deep-seated fears that involve rivalry that are part of
their personal histories. Some students express a fear of failure
when what they are really afraid of is success. Academic success
represents for such people a way of diminishing, or triumphing
over, people close to them, such as an ailing or unemployed parent,
or a sibling who has not had the potential or the opportunity to do
so well.

A student came to see a counsellor because, for the first
time in his life, he was having panic attacks. He had all the
classic symptoms – palpitations, sweaty palms, breathlessness.
These had begun to appear a few weeks earlier when he
was about to enter an underground station. Now he could
not travel anywhere by tube.
    The counsellor was concerned to understand why these

panic attacks had begun now. There seemed no obvious incident or reason that could explain their sudden onset. She was aware that it was the time of the year when students on this particular course went on work experience, and began to explore with the student whether there might be any connection. She also bore in mind that it might be an early manifestation of examination anxiety. As the sessions developed and she heard the family history, she helped the student make the connections which eventually alleviated his immediate anxiety.

Two years earlier, the student's brother had been killed in a car accident, just before he was about to take his final examinations in law at university. This brother had been seen as the cleverest one in the family and was the hope of his working class parents for a bright future. They decided to bury their son near his university but did not allow this student to attend his brother's funeral. No-one was allowed to speak of the dead brother at home.

During his sessions, a great deal of delayed grieving had to be worked through. What became clear as time went on was the student's fear of being successful. At an unconscious level he felt that, in being successful he would be killing his brother all over again. He did not dare to take his place as the more successful member of the family. That place belonged to his brother, who was no longer there to compete. How could he dare to win in such an unfair competition?

This is an example of both how examinations can represent an unconscious and denied part of the self, and how the fear of examinations can manifest itself at any time of the year. Since there was time to deal with the panic attacks, the student was able to succeed in his examinations. Sadly, his parents did not come to see him collect his award.

When students present themselves just before or during examinations, a more immediate way has to be found to deal with the impending crisis. Counsellors can employ a number of techniques, such as relaxation exercises, encouraging students to test the reality of how much they do in fact know, and using imagery to put students in touch with their worst fears. They may help them to find support outside counselling, referring some students for medication. Occasionally, counsellors have to be very active in order to help students to marshal their resources. At other times what is required is a sense of peace and calm in the presence of panic. For some students, the essential requirement is that somebody holds them in mind during this difficult period. This may be enough to sustain them and allow them to keep their own mind and thinking intact.

It is also possible to deal with deeply submerged material in a few sessions at a time of crisis. Ann Heyno (1994), head of the Counselling and Advisory Service at the University of Westminster, gives an example of counselling that encapsulates many of the principles outlined in this chapter. She describes how Lucy was brought to the counselling service by a tutor after she had walked out of an examination. She could not understand what had happened. Her mind had gone blank in the middle of her best paper. Heyno saw Lucy briefly to try to make sense of what had happened and to identify whether she needed to see a doctor. A longer appointment was made for two days later and Lucy was seen four times in total.

During the second session, Lucy talked of a recurring dream she had had the night before about her dead aunt, in which they were driving in a car. The car had stopped suddenly and the aunt had got out without saying goodbye. It later emerged that the day of the examination had been the fifth anniversary of the aunt's death; Lucy had been taking an examination on the day that her aunt had been killed in a road accident. In addition, she had not been allowed to go to the funeral because her parents had insisted that she sat an examination on that day as well. Heyno continues:

At this point, it was becoming increasingly clear to me that there was a connection between her feelings about her aunt's death and the current exam incident. The question in my mind was why now when she was doing so well? So far she had been successful on the course. At a conscious level, she wasn't thinking about her aunt, who had been very special to her and had lived with the family and looked after her when she was small. Indeed she felt that five years on she should have been over the death. But clearly she wasn't. Consciously she wasn't aware of a problem but her unconscious, first in the form of a dream and later in the blanking out in the exam, was a communication that something was seriously wrong. What she was unable to express consciously was expressing itself in action – in a symptom, exam anxiety. This conversion of anxiety into action is commonly referred to as 'acting out' – the self destructive act of spoiling her achievements in her best exam. Her conscious wish was to pass the exam, but her unconscious wish was to say, 'Hey, something is wrong. I am still deeply upset by my aunt's death and I am very angry that I wasn't allowed to go to the funeral and have the opportunity of saying goodbye'. Remember that in the dream, the aunt leaves without saying goodbye, which in reality is what happened through her sudden death.

My client's unresolved grief about her aunt's death and her anger with her parents for not acknowledging this, was being acted out as exam panic. Exams and bereavement had somehow become connected in her unconscious mind. A tentative comment linking the aunt's death and the exam panic brought my client great relief.

(Heyno 1994: 235)

In the next session, it emerged that Lucy had always underachieved in examinations since the death of her aunt, but had never walked out of an examination before. Heyno suggests that it was precisely because she was about to do well that she acted out her feelings of anger and loss. Lucy felt that her aunt had been the only one in the family who had valued her and believed in her abilities. When she was not there to see her do well, it was even more upsetting than usual. Because she could not express these feelings directly, she acted them out.

By the final session, Lucy was talking about feeling more aggressive than she ever had felt in her life. Her anger at her aunt for leaving her and at her parents for not allowing her to go to the funeral was now being expressed at a more conscious level. She had also persuaded her mother, who still did not understand why she had walked out of the examination, to take her to the crematorium where her aunt had been cremated. There she had imagined her aunt telling her that she was doing well. She felt great relief.

Heyno comments that she had observed that Lucy had a difficult relationship with her mother who had not gone to university. She felt that Lucy had a strong sense of rivalry with her mother coupled with guilt that she was doing better than her. This may also have accounted for Lucy's unresolved grief coming to the surface at a time when she was doing well. However, a tentative comment to this effect left Lucy unmoved. Heyno observes that even if there were unresolved issues about parental rivalry, Lucy did not want to consider them. This was not what she was asking for. She had wanted to know why she had walked out of the examination room and now felt that she understood. Indeed, she went on to complete her course successfully.

EATING DISORDERS

The difficulties experienced by people with eating disorders are well known, particularly because of the attention they receive in the media. While accepted as a fact of life, eating disorders can lead to death. Students in such a chronic state are usually under the care of the health services and not the counselling services. But the deadness in the lives of students with eating problems who do seek help from counsellors is, paradoxically, very much alive. It is this paradox and ambiguity, the use of food, in both a symbolic and real way, that could give life, to deaden the pain of living, which is so powerful.

The sociological and psychological imperatives of starving or bingeing and purging are well known (see Orbach 1978). For many years, the subject has been central to the women's movement and many female students who present with this problem confirm that they still feel the pressure to become the perfect woman. However, anecdotal evidence suggests that more male students are appearing at counselling services with problems connected with food. While at this point in time we do not have a detailed understanding of this, it is important to recognize that it is happening. It would appear that the commonly held belief that a woman's preoccupation with her body can develop into abusive dietary regimes, whereas a man's develops into punitive sporting schedules, is beginning to break down. Women are becoming compulsive gym users and men are becoming compulsive eaters. The shifts in society's demands as to how women and men should be are making themselves felt.

Issues of control and competitiveness are at the heart of some people's eating problem, and this can be exacerbated in educational settings. For adolescents in particular, the matter of who takes control of their lives is a constant struggle. The drive for separation is set against the need to be looked after and to remain a child rather than become an adult. Educational establishments can compound this confusion by expecting students to be autonomous and self-directed, while at the same time setting uncompromising timetables that require students to be dependent on the learning process. Being away from home for the first time, perhaps with limited finance, is another aspect of the educational setting that can contribute to an unhealthy need in students for a spurious kind of control.

Eating and learning: a mixed metaphor

The educational environment may have an impact on those with eating problems in one very specific way. Eating and learning problems can both be symbols in the present of past difficulties. When they come together in one person, the mixed symbols – or meta-phors – can be very powerful. Counsellors are then required to exhibit great skill either in disentangling the metaphors, or in working with the metaphors simultaneously because they stand for one and the same thing.

It is not coincidental that metaphors used to describe learning are drawn from our experiences of being nourished. We talk of taking in and digesting, chewing on an idea, regurgitating material in an examination. These metaphors are powerful because they describe learning in a way that associates us with our earliest dependent relationships. Among people with eating disorders, it is possible to see their relationship to learning vividly demonstrated in their re-lationship to food. Students who control their intake of food may also be saying something about the fear of digesting academic material served up on a daily basis. They can often be found in libraries rather than in lecture theatres making up their own limited aca-demic recipes and deciding for themselves how much they will absorb. That their lives become impoverished or that they might be undernourished academically is of no consequence to them, provid-ing they have sole control over what they take in.

Students who have a tendency to binge and purge can also be difficult to teach. They can give the appearance of being keen and may seem to be devouring every word the lecturer has to say, but when they leave the public arena they find that they cannot hold on to what they have learned. For some the range of the academic menu is too great. They cannot make a choice but feel that they have to gobble up every morsel put in front of them. When they come to counselling services, they have to be helped to differentiate between what is necessary, what will bring pleasure and what can be left to one side.

As with all difficulties experienced by students, examinations can be the focus that illustrates the depth of a problem. If students feel that they are being forced to cram everything in at once, then the examination period can become a very powerful mixed metaphor. An anorexic student commented that, since she felt almost everything was out of her control at examination time, at least she could control her eating. Because examinations can represent the end of adoles-cence, those whose eating problems are bound up with not wanting to become an adult will experience examinations as a time of crisis.

The practice of dealing with eating disorders

Student counsellors work in a variety of ways with people with eat-ing disorders. Many are influenced by models that focus on thinking and behaviour (Fairburn and Cooper 1989). Students, either individually or in groups, are helped to identify which aspects of their thinking and feeling affect their behaviour and to develop strategies for change. There is an impetus to improve students' self-image and self-esteem so that they have less need to denigrate themselves and their bodies. Other counsellors focus on early relationships and their significance. Ann Lindsay, the eating disorders specialist at Oxford University, suggests that a useful way to work is to concentrate on the dynamic of the relationship in the room. Can the student take in what is being offered? Are they able to make use of the material between sessions or do they come back each week empty, and desperate for a good feed? As in all counselling in education, there are times when the experience of being a student is addressed and an attempt is made to understand what impact this has on the individual.

Richards and McKisack (1993) and Ross (1993) have shown how students can be helped within a group setting at Birmingham and Reading universities, respectively. At Birmingham, a group of eight women meet for one ninety-minute session per week for eight weeks. Each session begins and ends with the members of the group taking it in turn to complete a common statement, for example 'One thing I like about the person next to me is . . .', or 'One thing I do well is . . .'. This round of comments helps group cohesion but also addresses the fundamental issue of self-esteem in a direct way. The sessions contain a mixture of group discussion, group exercises, work in groups of two or three and formal fact-giving talks by the convenors.

Throughout the sessions, the role of women in society is addressed. Particular attention is given to the way women are expected to conform to an idealized image. Richards and McKisack report that one of the most revealing exercises was a round which began, 'As a woman I am expected to . . .'. The women's responses, which included 'to be thin', 'to eat up all my food', 'not to get angry' and 'to be attractive', paved the way for an exploration of the feelings of anger surrounding these pressures and the way that feelings are, or are not, expressed.

A second theme is the impact of families and relationships with parents. This is explored through the medium of fantasy exercises (e.g. focusing on family meals). Richards and McKisack report that a wealth of powerful material emerges during these sessions. One woman began to realize that she had always taken second helpings at meal-times as a way of giving silent support to her mother. She went on to discover ways of providing support for her mother that did not bring her such personal distress.

At Reading University, similar methods are used, but in addition each client receives a 'self-help' pack. This provides them with a method for identifying and changing the thinking processes that trigger or maintain their behaviour. The pack contains a form that has to be filled in each week. It asks clients to list positive things about themselves and other members of the group. This technique also addresses issues of self-esteem. Counsellors at both universities report how difficult this is for group members, and Ross describes the excuses used to avoid completing this part of the exercise:

> One of the most crucial functions of the counsellor is to prevent this avoidance, and to ensure that self esteem statements are shifted from eating orientated attributions ('I am good because I managed to stop myself eating after my initial binge mouthful by telling myself, "yes it really does matter"') to other ones ('I am good because I managed to hang on to my integrity when arbitrating between my flat mates').
>
> (Ross 1993: 273)

At both universities, the Eating Disorder Inventory (Garner and Olmstead 1983) is used to assess students' progress. At Birmingham, an additional measure is implemented to identify students' sense of self-esteem (Rosenberg 1965). In both universities the groups were shown to be effective in maintaining change some months after the groups stopped meeting. This is encouraging to counsellors who work with students who have spent many years being obsessed by food.

SUICIDE AND SELF-HARM

As early as 1910, a symposium was organized in Vienna entitled 'On suicide with particular reference to suicide amongst young students'. The speakers included Freud, Adler and Stekel. While speculation in the modern press can in no way be compared with the challenging contributions of Freud and his colleagues, media coverage of student deaths in 1992–94 shows that preoccupation with the link between students and suicide has not abated.

A study by Hawton et al. (1995a) showed that, over a fourteen-year period, the overall number of student suicides at Oxford University (as defined by coroners' verdicts) was higher than that among people of the same age in the general population. However, when open verdicts were taken into account – a large proportion of which are likely to be suicides – this difference all but disappeared. This is the first major study of student suicide rates since the 1970s, prompted by the concern of Oxford University's Committee on Student Health at the apparently high number of student suicides in the late 1980s. They were somewhat reassured by the results of the survey, and while still concerned about the death of any young person, recognized that the belief that students were more prone than others to suicide is unfounded.

Hawton et al. (1995b) also compared the number of attempted suicides among Oxford University students with those among their peers in the general population in the City of Oxford. They found a lower rate among the students, which may be linked to such factors as socio-economic class. However, Hawton and his colleagues stated that 'the invaluable supportive environment and pastoral care offered by colleges, as well as the invaluable contributions of Nightline and the University Counselling Service, do indeed benefit students and especially those whose personal lives are impaired by emotional or psychological problems'.

Of particular interest is the fact that ten of the twenty-one students who committed suicide did so outside Oxford and that nine of them did so during vacations. In addition, ten of the students had psychiatric disorders, eight of whom were undergoing treatment at the time of their deaths. It was also reported that a large proportion of the students who attempted suicide failed to take up the offer of aftercare at the hospital which had dealt with them at the point of crisis. It was suggested that they might find aftercare offered through the counselling service more acceptable.

Despite these two reports, student suicides are a major preoccupation in colleges and universities throughout Britain. This is apparent both in informal and formal conversations. It is impossible to halt all acts of suicide and even where the best facilities are available, some students will not seek help during moments of desperation. Nevertheless, there lingers the hope that counselling services will save universities and colleges from such tragedies.

In recent years student counselling services have been asked more often what arrangements they have in place for emergencies and at weekends. While this might be a legitimate question, there is often a false assumption that if services were to remain open at all times, suicides would not occur. This unrealistic and often unconscious demand places extra pressure on counsellors, who therefore have to be clear within themselves about what they can and what they cannot do. Counselling services are not emergency services. Nor can counsellors be omnicompetent and omnipresent. As the next chapter suggests, this is one area where it is important for counsellors to work with other members of the institution to develop a realistic understanding of what is possible.

Because there was a cluster of sudden student deaths at Oxford University during 1992–94, the counselling service developed a way of working with members of colleges where deaths had occurred. Based on a developing understanding of the needs of people after traumatic incidents, the counsellors make themselves available to members of colleges on site. They help colleges to identify who may need support: those who may have been immediately involved (e.g. those who found the body); close friends and academic colleagues; students or staff who may be vulnerable for other reasons and for whom a sudden death may be an additional difficulty; or senior members of staff dealing with the family of the student who has died or with the Press. At all times, counsellors see their central task as supporting members of the college who are already managing the process. They do not see themselves as the experts who come in and take over. Experience has shown the counsellors that there are a number of highly skilled members of colleges who know what is right for their particular students in their setting. However, when it is felt appropriate by the college, counsellors offer specialized help. One of the most powerful experiences for counsellors has been in facilitating groups for close friends and colleagues of a student who has died. In this way, they can help them make personal sense of an event that appears to make no sense at all.

This example of counsellors, students, academic and administrative staff working together, each respecting the other's area of expertise and knowledge, serves as a model for cooperation throughout the academic year. The need to liaise and work with other members of the institution and with other professionals is very much part of student counsellors' everyday experience. How this takes place forms the core of Chapter 5.

· FIVE ·

Professional relationships in student counselling

Where counselling takes place in any organizational setting, there is a web of professional relationships which is both overt and hidden. There are inevitable hierarchies and subtle distributions of power and influence that can take years for a member of an organization to fathom. For some counsellors who choose to work quietly behind closed doors, the idea of trying to locate the power and influence in an institution is anathema. If within the field of education they resist doing this, they will find that in a practical sense they place their services at a disadvantage, for example in decisions about funding. Equally importantly, they fail to understand the context in which their clients function. Student counsellors must have a relationship with the broader institution and its structures.

In smaller establishments, a counsellor may have a seat on policy-making committees. Bringing a counselling perspective to decision making can benefit both the institution as well as the counselling service itself. Elsewhere, where there is resistance to counselling having a formal place within the committee structure, counsellors have used the democratic process to get elected to appropriate committees; for example, by becoming staff representatives on academic boards and governing bodies. When the latter is the case they need to be clear about their constituency and to know when there are conflicting needs. In both these instances of representation, colleagues see counselling in a different light and begin to appreciate what individual counsellors may have to offer.

It is ironic that counsellors in further education are often envious of the prestige that they imagine their colleagues in higher education enjoy. In reality, the larger and more prestigious the institution, the more difficult it is for counsellors to have a direct impact on policy formulation. Where there is integrated student services provision, the route to decision making is through the head of student services, who is rarely a counsellor. While relationships with this person may be good, his or her brief is on behalf of student services as a whole, leading to competition for resources and influence. In more traditional establishments, the route to decision making is often through many layers of committees comprised of eminent and long-serving members. Because of the way most counselling services are placed within the structure, the chances of counsellors finding a constituency from which to be elected to committees within these traditional establishments is minimal.

It is becoming increasingly important, at a time when all institutions are constrained by funding implications, that counselling services should be familiar with the prevailing ethos in senior management. They may not agree with it, but they need to know its likely impact on their work.

TUTORS AND TEACHING COLLEAGUES

While face-to-face contact with senior management may be sporadic, each day counsellors have to liaise with those who have primary responsibility for the development of students. These contacts range from the preliminary enquiry from tutors as to whether a student is in need of referral, to the longer-term contact through shared interest in a student's progress. The process of referral is spelled out in more detail below, but here it is important to consider the nature of the links between tutoring, teaching and counselling.

There is much confusion in academic institutions about the role of personal tutors, much of it centred on the question, 'How much of a counsellor is the tutor expected to be?' This question underlines the anxiety in academics' minds that they are being asked to take on a role for which they have not been trained and a task that will take them into personal areas of their students' lives that might be fraught with hidden dangers.

Personal tutoring is part of the traditional role of the academic tutor in the older universities, where teaching had usually been on a one-to-one basis. More recently, it has been added to by the development of personal and social education in schools and colleges. The underlying concept is that performance in an academic institution is not just about academic knowledge or skills that need to be acquired, but also involves feelings and emotions. However, there is not always agreement about how to effect this concept.

Definitions of tutoring and descriptions of the tutorial practice vary. A number of counselling services have attempted to address these issues by producing handbooks for use within the institution (Sheffield University), videotapes of tutorial sessions (Birmingham University) and training sessions in tutorial skills (North East Surrey College of Technology). Wheeler and Birtle (1993), in *A Handbook for Personal Tutors*, draw on their experience of being tutors in higher education and on Wheeler's former work as the student counsellor at Aston University, where she was closely involved in the training and support of personal tutors. Bramley (1977), in *Personal Tutoring in Higher Education*, wrote of a need to create within institutions a 'nourishing environment'. It would appear that the role of the personal tutor is to assist in providing for the needs of students beyond the straightforward teaching which we have traditionally expected academic tutors to provide.

In many institutions, the role of the academic tutor and the personal tutor are quite separate. The view is that students and tutors alike would not be able to cope with the conflict of roles the merging of these two functions would engender. When these roles are separated, then personal tutors are in fact being asked, in some respects, to act as personal counsellors, and to respond in ways for which, in most cases, they usually have not been trained. They are being asked to be non-judgemental, non-assessing and, they may therefore feel, non-academic. Those who have worked within this model know just how difficult it is to operate.

A second model requires that all academic tutors should be personal tutors. It suggests an ideal situation where the lecturer/tutor possesses a variety of skills and experience, and is able to offer the student a comprehensive and completely fulfilling learning environment. However, when seen in practice, there is often an underlying assumption that there are no differences between the skills of lecturing and personal tutoring. Frequently, the focus of the relationship becomes entirely academic, with anything of a personal nature referred to a professional counsellor. This looks like a much safer model: each to his or her own task and each staying with what he or she knows best. Sadly, this can lead to a one-dimensional view of the student by the tutor and of the tutor by the student. It leads also to massively overcrowded counselling services.

A third model is that personal tutoring falls somewhere between these two extremes, that it includes both the academic and the personal and that it involves skills peculiar to itself. It recognizes that students may be supported most appropriately by someone who teaches them, but it also recognizes that personal tutoring involves a different kind of relationship and a different mode of operation. Even within this model, the term 'personal tutor' causes some confusion and anxiety (because of what 'personal' is seen to mean). The task of the tutor is to hold an overview of students' progress, both academically and socially. It is to keep students in view, and from that perspective to make clear to them that they are recognized and known personally. What cannot be over-emphasized is the value to students of being 'known'. The feeling of not being known and therefore feeling not valued is a dominant one in the presentations of students who come to formal counselling services. They may give the impression of no longer wishing for or needing a parent to keep watch over them, and indeed sometimes appear to be hostile to anyone who dares to offer such support, but below the surface they are often longing to be made to feel 'at home'. Fisher (1994), in her work on student stress, shows homesickness to be a dominant theme and that transition to university is a stressful event for all who undertake it.

If it is accepted that the task of the tutor is to 'know' the student then personal tutoring can be defined in the following ways:

1 It is first and foremost a developmental task, not a problem-oriented one.
2 It contains an identifiable academic component where issues to do with the learning process are monitored.
3 It is the place where the reality of the environment is attended to by both tutor and student.
4 It is akin to the parent–child relationship, where the student is held and contained in a natural way.
5 It offers the opportunity for creative play, during which the student explores the inner and outer worlds; the link between subjectivity and objectivity.

If these are the functions of personal tutoring, then it can be seen that the tutor is called upon to adopt a variety of roles. Ellen Noonan in discussions on tutoring clearly defines these roles as:

1 *Mentor and patron* – offering personal knowledge and generosity of experience.
2 *Advocate* – representing the student in places where he or she can't go.
3 *Prosecutor* – representing the demands and resources of the institution to the student.
4 *Partner* – sharing and discovering together, whether about academic or social matters.

5 *Student* – learning from and being excited by new ideas generated
   by the student.
6 *Anchor* – being a stable point of reference in confusion and being
   a point of departure for the student's exploration of the unknown world.

Given all these roles, it is clear why tutoring as a whole is so
difficult to sustain. In a climate of increased pressure on academic
staff, it may appear to be impossible. Noonan refers to an 'agility of
relationships' that are inherent in the tutoring role. However, she
does not include in her list the term 'counsellor' and this seems to
answer the all-important question. Without doubt tutors may well
employ advanced counselling skills when carrying out their other
roles and functions; but the formal role of counsellor (Chapter 2) is
one that is very rarely asked for or required. On rare occasions
when it is, tutors have a right if they wish to explain that this
request takes them outside their experience and training, and to
gently but firmly refer to someone who is known and trusted.

It can be liberating for tutors to know that they do not have to
take on a formal counselling role unless they wish; and that, equally
importantly, it is usually inappropriate for them to do so. It frees
tutors to do what they do best, to work within their many and
differing roles and to know that they can retain their identity and
purpose as academics, who have taken particular care both to understand and stand alongside students as they grow and develop.

In one FE college, where tutoring was less clearly defined, a tutor
got himself into serious difficulties by losing sight of the boundaries
within his role. He began by befriending a bright student who showed
considerable academic potential, but who came from an emotionally abusive family with whom he still lived. The tutor offered the
student extra tutorial time because he was falling behind with his
work, but before long the sessions had turned from one where the
focus was on work, to lengthy 'counselling' sessions about the student's difficulties within his family. The student began to demand
more time of the tutor and still little academic work was being
done. Eventually, the tutor rang the counselling service. He was
exhausted, demoralized and felt criticized by his colleagues, who
were tired of the excuses he made on behalf of the student who
had still done no work. He felt abused. When the counsellor saw
the student, he too was demoralized. The tutor had seemed to offer
something the student had never experienced before: he had been
offered encouragement and support, and he had been offered time
(the tutor had given the student his home telephone number saying,

'Ring me if you need to' but had seemed to the student off-hand when he rang one Saturday night). But all this now seemed false. The student felt rejected and deceived by the referral to the counselling service by someone he thought he could trust. He felt that what he had to say was unbearable to the tutor and that he, himself, could not be tolerated. What began so productively turned out for the student to be a repetition of his sense of being abused.

To the tutor's credit, he later telephoned the counselling service and asked for some time to think about what had gone wrong. He said that he not only needed to think about his role as a tutor, but that he also needed to understand why what he thought of as helpful counselling had become so unmanageable.

COUNSELLING SKILLS TRAINING FOR COLLEAGUES

Experienced counsellors are a major resource to their institutions when they are prepared to offer training in counselling skills to their colleagues, whether at a basic or more advanced level. As they become more confident in these skills, they also recognize the limits of their expertise, and are able to refer to a specialist centre when more profound issues need to be addressed. It is important that counsellors recognize where these skills are already being used and take initiatives to enhance them, rather than become precious about their definition of counselling and fiercely territorial.

The most frequent problem is that although many individuals express the desire for training, they show less willingness or ability to commit themselves to regular sessions. Counsellors then find themselves in a quandary about whether or not to appear to collude with the notion that counselling skills can be learned in an irregular and piecemeal fashion. Many are pragmatic and, with careful explanation of how the training might equip course members, take the opportunity to develop a counselling awareness in their colleagues.

Counsellors have found ways of helping their colleagues add a new perspective to their work. Courses are offered to a broad range of people: tutors and lecturers, administrative staff, librarians, porters and domestic staff (who are often among the first to spot students in trouble), and colleagues in the welfare services. Although the number of course members in any one year may be small, the accumulative and cascade effect of people returning to their faculties and departments with a confidence and belief in what they are doing is beneficial to the students, the institution and the counselling service.

Peer support training

For many years, counsellors in a number of institutions have worked with members of student groups to develop their awareness of issues facing other students. This is done by organizing occasional sessions with students' unions and mature students' societies. These sessions broaden their understanding, give them some warning of what they might expect to find as they take up leading roles in the institution, and introduce them to the facilities of counselling services. They are essentially briefing sessions that help to form useful relationships between student groups and counsellors, making the process of cross-referral easier. However, some counsellors have tried to introduce a more systematic form of training for students in an attempt to increase their capacity to cope with issues that are brought to them.

Chris Hodgkinson (1993) describes a training programme that has been set up at the University of Ulster to assist students involved in the induction of new students. This practice of mentoring is to be found in many universities and colleges. By giving students basic training in listening skills, alerting them to the issues with which they might be confronted, and offering support sessions, Hodgkinson has formalized a process that is often carried out on an *ad hoc* basis. Since settling into a new institution can be a difficult experience, it seems sensible that second- and third-year students who take responsibility for 'freshers' should be given some understanding of the process, and so know why and what they are doing. This programme has a specific task and clear limits and boundaries. However, the skills learned are not forgotten and may well be used by students in other ways as they progress through university.

Whenever students are asked informally or in more structured surveys where they go to find help, the answer is always that they turn, in the first instance, to other students or friends. Although not surprising, one of the consequences of this is that many students carry around the burdens of their friends. In order to address this issue, Oxford University Counselling Service has offered undergraduates a 36-hour course in basic counselling skills since 1990. The programme runs once or twice a year, depending on the resources available. In 1994, a separate course was introduced for graduate students who have a clearly defined pastoral role. The primary aim of these courses is to give students confidence in their ability to help other students, while at the same time giving them permission to set firm boundaries. The decision to call the programme 'Peer Support Training' rather than, for example, 'An Introduction to Counselling', was a deliberate one. The title of the course reflects the task, that students should remain as friends and colleagues who temporarily employ counselling skills to help others when in difficulty.

The course teaches them to listen attentively, to ask open-ended questions that will encourage further communication, to resist giving an opinion inappropriately, and to look for the feelings behind the words. But as well as practising what might be described in other spheres as good communication skills, students are asked to think about the particular significance of what is being communicated within the context of the helping role they have assumed. Why have they been chosen to hear this particular problem and what is the expectation of what might happen next? Students are gently introduced to the idea that those who seek help may have unrealistic expectations and those who offer help might equally expect the impossible of themselves. Exercises are used to draw on the students' own experiences. In this way, they see that a specific situation can produce a variety of personal responses and thus they can begin to differentiate between their own experience and that of others. The topics covered, such as family relationships and dealing with prejudice, produce much personal material. Although the primary task is not to be a therapy group, many of the students talk openly about these issues for the first time. While time is allowed for these feelings to be heard and acknowledged, the course convenor always brings them back to the focus of the training: What was it like to talk in such a way? How did it feel? What are the implications of this for work with other students? The most powerful sessions are those that deal with crisis management and issues about supporting students who have suicidal ideas. The relief that these can be talked about is enormous. It is equally important that strategies for coping in such situations are offered. Two weeks after one course had ended, a student was called on to help another student who was suicidal. He went to his file from the course and read quickly through what he had learned. What he had been taught was relevant in a practical way; he had conveyed an air of confidence and calm to other students who were attempting to help their distressed friend. Most importantly, he later said that he knew that he should contact other people: it was not he alone who was responsible for the safety of the student.

After the course, students are offered limited follow-up sessions on a regular basis where they can talk about issues that have arisen. Some students make it clear to their colleagues that they have done the training and that they are available to help. Others prefer to use their new skills in a completely informal way. Whatever the chosen mode of operation, each has the opportunity of the limited group supervision sessions, and access to a counsellor by telephone should they need it.

These courses are always over-subscribed, thus indicating a real need for them. A number of colleges have bought in the services of the trainer to run in-house training. This is often geared not just to students, but to a welfare committee of academics, administrative staff and students. The benefit to the counselling service is that more people are aware of how it functions and, more specifically, students who have attended these peer support programmes are able to make sound and appropriate referrals.

REFERRAL PROCEDURES

In all sectors of student counselling, the most common route is via self-referral (ASC 1995), followed by referral from tutors and lecturers (particularly in further education). In higher education, another common referral route is through medical centres. The fact that a majority of students are self-referred has implications for the kind of services required, since there is very little filtering of clients. This means that student counsellors need good assessment skills (see Chapter 3). When a referral is made by another person, it is often from someone who has had little first-hand experience of counselling. Such people need to be shown what counselling can and cannot do.

When a referral takes place, at least three people are always involved, which allows for positive collaboration or for negative and competitive collusion. Each person brings to the process certain expectations and fears that will influence the success of the referral and which, where possible, need to be checked. The most common question asked of student counsellors by their academic colleagues is, 'How do I know whether someone should be referred to you?' This encapsulates the desire to get it right and the fear that they may get it wrong.

Some referrals are the result of desperation, due to the fact that everything has been tried but nothing has worked. The counselling service is seen as the last resort. When this happens, the counsellor may also find that the student cannot be helped and has the difficult task of explaining this to the referrer. Such students may not want to be in counselling or are unable to use a psychological approach to help them with their difficulty. Occasionally, they need to be referred on for psychiatric assessment; sometimes they need a more practical approach from one of the other welfare services. Although the constant process of 'educating' referrers helps, the proximity of student counselling services to mainstream educational activities means that the services attract both idealized and hostile projections from colleagues. Counsellors also have to guard against their own desires to be seen as able to deal with anything and anybody.

The most successful referrals are made when the referrer has taken some time to talk to the student, to discover something of the issue (without being intrusive), and has explored the student's feelings about being referred. If referrers also examine their own feelings about making a referral, this improves the chances of a successful outcome. It should not be such a rapid response that the student feels rejected, nor so late that the referrer and the student become entangled in the issues and their relationship. Students sometimes say that they feel better when referral is mentioned, just to convince the referrer that they do not need to be referred.

Occasionally referrals are not successful when the student and counsellor are unable to establish a working relationship. In long-term counselling it is recognized that early difficulties in a counselling relationship can be carried over from earlier relationships, and that these can be worked through. In short-term work, there is little time for the student and counsellor to work together on why the relationship appears to be unhelpful, and there is often a greater need to cooperate closely with referrers, to help deal with these early difficulties.

There are powerful dynamics at work in the referral procedure. The person referring may feel hope, desperation, reluctance, envy, gratitude and loss. Counsellors, for their part, may feel equally hopeful, desperate or reluctant, omnipotent or powerless, competent or unskilled. For students who are referred there are the usual feelings at the beginning of any new encounter, but in addition they may feel that they are pleasing an assessor, or that they are being rejected, or that their problem is so great that it cannot be dealt with normally.

A particularly powerful dynamic occurs when a student is 'sent' as part of a disciplinary procedure. Since counsellors believe that counselling should only take place if it is freely entered into, they are faced with a dilemma when students are told they *must* attend the counselling service. If a tutor has contacted the service in advance, there is at least the opportunity to explore the wisdom of such a referral. What happens most often, however, is that the reasons are revealed during an initial session, when the student is asked about their reasons for contacting the service or about their expectations of the process. If the student is there under duress, the counsellor may check the student's perception of the consequences of not doing as requested, or ask permission to contact the appropriate authority figures. Sometimes it is discovered that the student has not in fact been forced to come but that, more benignly, a strong recommendation has been made. Someone has recognized a troubled person beneath the trouble-maker. Nevertheless, the counsellor has to work with the student's perception and, if indeed an ultimatum has been delivered, the counsellor has to decide whether to comply with the demands of the institution or not.

A surprising amount of good counselling work can be done with students who have been confronted with the consequences of unacceptable behaviour or attitudes to work. Their appearance at the counselling service suggests that, however unconscious, there may be a wish for change. They could simply have left the institution. If they can be helped to articulate their wish to change, they are in a better position to make their own decision about whether or not counselling could be helpful.

> A male student said he had been sent to the counselling service because he had been violent towards his girlfriend on college premises. He had been subject to disciplinary procedures and had been told that he could stay on his course providing he came for counselling. He was still angry with the girl and his college and now he was angry with the counselling service.
>
> The counsellor said in a quite confrontational way, 'Well, you've done what you were told. You're here now. Are you going to use this chance to try to understand how you've got into this mess or are you going to fight it because you were told to come?' The student looked startled and then grinned. After checking out how confidential the counselling might be, he then began to work.
>
> After eight sessions of individual counselling, in which he began to understand in a profound way the complexities of his feelings about his family, his former friends and his ex-girlfriend, he asked the counsellor whether it might be possible for him to join a therapeutic group. This time there was no ambiguity about his wish to understand more and to change.

This student was able to use counselling to his benefit, despite being sent, but successful counselling may not signal the end of a dilemma for a counsellor. If a student's place on a course is conditional on an improvement in his or her behaviour or emotional state, who decides whether or not the student has been 'cured'? If a student has been allowed to remain on the course while the counselling is in process, it is to be hoped that there is some clear evidence to course organizers that the student has changed. However, some students are advised to take time off, particularly if they are very distressed. They are told they can return to their courses when they can provide evidence that they are in a fit state to continue. This evidence is usually requested in the form of a counsellor's report.

Broad issues of confidentiality were examined in Chapter 3, but during the referral process counsellors face specific difficulties in relation to confidentiality. This is particularly true when there is an expectation of a report. The more traditional view in counselling is that responsibility for transactions outside the therapeutic space, contained within the counselling relationship, rests with the client. The counsellor should not intervene in the client's life, since this will lead to contamination of the therapeutic process. Normally within this framework of understanding, a student counsellor will refuse to provide any kind of report. It can be argued, however, that the therapeutic space in education is wider than that between the student and counsellor. There is certainly a need to maintain confidentiality about what goes on in counselling sessions, but the process of agreeing what should go into a report can be therapeutic in itself. However, even within this broader framework of understanding, there is still the difficult problem if the institution is looking for proof of change. Counsellors can rarely offer certainty. In fact they offer the opposite – the possibility of living and working with uncertainty – but this is not welcome information when a report is requested.

The conflicts between student counsellors and their institutions about feedback to those who refer should not be underestimated. In at least one case, a counsellor felt it necessary to resign because she saw that her work with students was compromised by the institution's persistent demands for information. The controlling behaviour of the institution seemed to be based not on a need to hold the counsellor accountable or on a desire to help the students, but on an overwhelming anxiety about what they imagined might be going on behind the closed doors of the counsellor's room. With all referrals and requests for feedback, counsellors might ponder where the anxiety lies. This is particularly important when the request is for an immediate appointment with instant feedback, but it is equally valid when the request is more moderate and considered.

Tutors who are working successfully with students they wish to refer may need reassurance that what they are doing is appropriate, and that they have access to support when and if they need it. Offering this kind of support and liaison work makes counselling part of the day-to-day life of the college or university and demonstrates that counselling concepts and insights have a relevance beyond the confines of the counselling room. This is not just important for students, tutors and counsellors engaged in therapeutic work, but can be a foundation for negotiation when inevitable institutional dynamics, and even rivalries, begin to appear.

RELATIONSHIPS WITH ALLIED PROFESSIONALS WITHIN STUDENT SERVICES

Institutions tend to have clearer policies about parts of the guidance, welfare and advisory provision which they can see as having a more measurable outcome. Thus, for example, careers services, accommodation bureaux and, increasingly, financial services tend to be better resourced than counselling services. There is some logic to this policy, as most students use careers services, whereas only a minority use counselling services. But this understandably can cause feelings of envy. For example, counsellors envy the large number of staff on careers teams, whereas members of careers teams envy the amount of time that counsellors spend with their students. Welfare advisers can envy the counsellors' role, title and status, and counsellors can look longingly at the more practical, and clearly useful help on offer in welfare services. All services, including the well resourced, frequently feel that they do not have enough to do the job properly, and in their worst moments they may imagine that the other sections of student services have gained at their expense. However, within this potentially difficult situation there are many issues in common and many opportunities for liaison.

Careers services

There is a dynamic at work in all career choices, including the nursery nurse who needs to be looked after and the geographer who is trying to find a place in the world. Work can represent deep and unconscious needs, needs that can often be met successfully when a student's career choice and personal needs are congruent. It is when these are in conflict that students get into difficulty. This is why careers and counselling services need to work closely together, so that careers advisers can refer students to counsellors when it seems impossible for them to make healthy, conscious choices about their future.

A careers adviser spoke to a counsellor about a student who had been having great difficulty following up information offered on the careers she wished to consider. At times the student would say, 'I think I would really like to be a teacher (or a librarian, or work in personnel)' and then would say that after all she didn't think she would be any good at it. The adviser was beginning to piece together information about the student's earlier life and suspected that the student's confidence in her own ability had been damaged by very controlling parents. She wanted to know whether she should refer the student for counselling.

The counsellor asked whether the adviser had any evidence that the student could make some links with her past, pointing out that if she could not, then he, as a counsellor, was unlikely to make any more progress with the student than the adviser had done. He suggested some simple questions the adviser might ask of the student in order to assess whether she was able to move into a more therapeutic approach to understanding her inability to make a career choice. They agreed that they would talk after the adviser's next session with the student, when the student's answers would help them both to decide whether counselling might be of help.

Conversely, counsellors may need to refer students to careers services in order that they can test out the reality of what the future might hold and what it might be possible to do.

A student was referred to a counselling service because both her tutor and her doctor were worried that she was extremely depressed and potentially suicidal. She was at the end of her first term in the college. She felt that she could not cope with the course and its demands and that she had made a wrong choice.

During the counselling sessions, it emerged that she felt there was nothing else that she could do and that death was the only way out. There were many powerful issues to be dealt with, including her complicated relationships with her family, who had been influential in her choice of course, and her perceptions of herself as someone for whom there was no future. What she also needed was evidence of what someone with qualifications such as hers might be able to do. A telephone call to the careers service ensured that she would be dealt with by an adviser who would present the information in a gentle but realistic way; she would not be given too much information at a time when she was so vulnerable, but she would be allowed to see that there were possible alternatives to death.

In subsequent sessions, the counsellor was able to use the student's response to the information to deepen the therapeutic work.

The counsellor in this case was fortunate because he had a good relationship with the careers service and knew which of the staff might be most helpful. In addition, a protocol had been agreed between the two services in order to deal with situations such as this. The student did not have to wait for an appointment and the careers adviser was happy to take on board the counsellor's suggestions as to what might be an appropriate way of handling the student's enquiry. Within the code of confidentiality, no unnecessary information was shared, but enough was said to allow each professional to act in the student's best interests.

Such inter-professional relationships are more difficult if there is little or no formal contact between the two services or if there are competing views about appropriate helping strategies. In the new universities, such an integration of student service provision is more possible. In the old universities, however, there have been few opportunities to meet within the formal structure of the institution. Instead, contacts have been made on a personal basis. In FE colleges, careers guidance has been provided by LEA careers services, which has allowed little opportunity for real liaison work. With the introduction of integrated services within further education, this issue has begun to be addressed. However, the picture in further education has been further complicated by the effective privatization in the early 1990s of LEA careers services. Now that colleges have to 'buy in' these services, they may be more able to choose the kind of personnel and service they require. It is equally possible that the agency providing the service is so preoccupied with the need to meet financial targets, and with performance indicators, that its staff are less inclined to spend time with students who are confused or in distress.

Student counsellors and careers advisers often share a common view of the impact of change on their client population, and may even have a shared theoretical base within their training. However, contacts between the two services are often minimal. Were more time and energy available, they might discover that a more consistent and creative alliance could be developed.

Financial and welfare services

Research carried out by the Cooperative Bank in 1994 showed that the average student at the end of a three-year undergraduate course was in debt to the tune of £2200. It is clear that good financial advice is essential for students at all levels of education if they are to complete their courses without feeling that the price has been too great.

The euphoria of getting into college or university often masks the necessity of financial planning. Unfortunately, some admissions tutors do not spell out the difficulties in precise detail, for fear that the student may be discouraged from joining the course. They, too, have financial realities to deal with. When seeking the help of a financial adviser, students often have unrealistic notions of what resources are available to help them, and the adviser has the difficult task of confronting them with the situation as it is, and not as they hoped it might be.

Some students start out with a financial plan and then discover that it does not work, or that their situation has changed so much that they can no longer manage. Each brings to the adviser a sense of outrage that they should be in such a situation and, frequently, a sense of panic and dread.

Advisers have to deal with these emotionally charged situations every day and too often they are left with little support or opportunity to explore the feelings aroused. When advisers, as in the case of the University of Westminster, are part of a combined counselling and advisory service, they are less isolated – the different experiences and expertise can be shared. Those who have a dual welfare and counselling role can often use supervision to understand the dynamics of the welfare work and are thus more able to cope. In counselling, if someone expresses anger at the counsellor there is usually an opportunity to work with this; to hold it for a time and then to hand it back appropriately. In advisory and welfare work, there is not the same mandate to work on emotional content, and advisers can find themselves the targets of feelings which might be more appropriately aimed elsewhere. They often have little opportunity to do anything more than hold on to feelings and make sure that they themselves do not retaliate. This may leave advisers full of other people's emotions with less and less time or energy to attend to their own.

In many instances, it is impossible for counsellors to do their job without the parallel facilities that financial and welfare advisers offer. Students cannot look at the more subtle reasons for their distress if they are worried that they are not going to survive on the course, or that they do not have enough money to buy food.

A mature student on a 'Preparation for work' course was referred to the counselling service by her tutors because she seemed to be permanently despondent. She had come to the country from an island in the Indian Ocean four years previously to marry someone she had known for a long time. After the birth of their son, her husband left home and the student had been trying to cope on her own for two years. She was determined to make a life for herself and her son, and she showed considerable potential on her course. However, she was not coping financially, and she was becoming unhealthy because she was existing on a restricted diet.

The counsellor helped her to talk about her sense of loss; about her warm island life where her family was well regarded and where there was never any lack of food; about her husband who had turned into someone she had never really known at all; and of her loss of self-esteem.

The welfare adviser, to whom the counsellor referred her, was able to offer twice weekly support for a time to help her manage her budget and to put her in touch with other single parents who shared her cultural background. In this way, not only did she find personal support, but she also learned how to cook less expensive meals.

Without the adviser's help, the counsellor would have had to deal with a woman whose daily experience was making her sad and unhealthy, and too preoccupied to deal with her underlying sense of loss. Without the counsellor, the adviser would have had great difficulty in persuading a woman who was grieving to make use of practical resources in the present. With the student's permission, they shared appropriate information and occasionally had joint meetings so that all three would have a realistic understanding of the stage they had reached in the process.

Sadly, counsellors often undervalue the work of advisers. This may be because counsellors feel the need to distinguish their counselling function from that of advising, and thus project the unwanted parts of their job onto advisers, whom they see as less sophisticated than themselves. Advisers can also see the less practical and the more student-centred ways that counsellors have of working as representing a wish of their own that they dare not, or do not have the time, to realize. These, or similar unconscious ways of regarding each other, mean that both counsellors and advisers have to guard against colluding with the splitting that goes on in any institution about the relative merits of services.

Generally, when they are not operating at the level of myth and stereotype, most student counsellors recognize that advisers deal with a large proportion of the student population at a time when they are at their most distressed. The skill and immediacy of this work is recognized. The use of counselling skills by both counsellors and advisers allows for a common ethical framework and belief in the value of students. Recognition of this fact would be of value not just to the two services and for relationships between them, but to the students as well. This might occur if counsellors and advisers met to discuss their work and to dispel the myths they have created about each other. Some student counselling services offer supervision to advisers; others include advisers in counsellors' team meetings. While these two models may not be acceptable to all counsellors and advisers, they demonstrate that constructive dialogue can take place.

Student unions

In addition to welfare and finance advisers, or where there is no welfare provision in the main institution, the student union has a major role to play in supporting students when in difficulty. Relationships between the various union officials and a counselling service are of vital importance. Some student unions employ their own welfare advisers in permanent posts and a small number (e.g. the London School of Economics) employ a counsellor. However, the welfare and advisory role, and occasionally that of counsellor, is usually carried out by elected union officials. These officials either have a sabbatical year from their studies or carry out these duties in addition to their studies. They are therefore usually young, untrained and enthusiastic, and this represents both a strength and a weakness in the system. Their caseload may be large and they often deal with complicated problems and disturbed students who do not wish to make contact with a counselling service.

A vice-president of a student union contacted the
counselling service because she was concerned about a
student whom she had just seen. He had come to ask about
the rules for changing courses. He had made a request to
his faculty but had been told that a move was out of the
question. The student union official knew that this was not
the case and had begun to think that the seemingly sensible,
but unhappy student was the victim of deliberate
misinformation. However, as her session with him
developed, she began to observe that the student
occasionally made illogical links in the conversation and
much later in the session became alarmed as his
observations became more bizarre.

She recognized that the student needed more help than
she was able to offer. She acknowledged how distressing the
student was finding the situation, and suggested he might be
helped through the counselling service. She said that if he
were willing to be referred, she would be able to remain in
contact with him and that she could deal with any practical
issues to do with his course. He refused to be referred,
saying that counsellors were evil and that they were only
there to make money out of you. She asked if she could
speak to his faculty and again he refused.

She was, by this time, desperately worried about her
capacity to cope and about the student's state of mental
health. She brought the session to a conclusion as quickly as
she could without making the student feel worse and then
telephoned the counselling service.

The counsellor talked to her about the session and
reassured her that she had acted appropriately. He helped
her to deal with her anxiety and her feelings that she
should immediately inform the faculty of the student's
condition. The counsellor asked her whether she thought
that the student was an immediate risk to himself or to
other students, and discovered that this appeared not to be
the case. He also asked her if she had any thoughts on why
the faculty was appearing to be difficult. She began to
realize that the faculty might already be aware of this
student's personality difficulties; and that even if this were
not the case, the student had left saying that he was going
to fight their decision, and they might well discover the
problem before long. She also began to understand her
feelings of helplessness and her need to be active. She

realized that to have any chance of making a referral in the future, she should not go against the student's veto on contacting his faculty.

The counsellor assured the union official that he would be available to help if needed, and agreed with her that if the student returned that she should attempt to restrict her sessions to information and practical advice. In this way, she might feel that she was working with what was familiar. She could stress the need for referral if the student attempted to take the discussion into more emotive areas.

Some weeks later the counsellor saw a student for an assessment session. As the session evolved the material seemed familiar. He later telephoned the student union official and checked if the student they had spoken of before was from a particular faculty. When the union official confirmed this, the counsellor suggested that she might be relieved to know that the student had come for counselling. No details of what the student had said were shared, but the counsellor was able to tell her that she had been right in her assessment that the student was not a risk to himself or to others, and that it was unlikely that he would break down immediately. The counsellor did not see this as breaking confidentiality, since no information about the student was revealed other than to tell the union officer that her referral had eventually been successful.

In some services, counsellors offer supervision to student union welfare officers and to women's officers, who frequently carry a heavy welfare caseload. The main task of these sessions is to de-velop their skills but also to help them to draw boundaries. Often they intuitively respond well but need reassurance to trust their own judgement.

A relatively new student union welfare officer rang a counsellor, who was her supervisor, because she felt that she could not wait until the next session to discuss a student whom she had just referred to the counselling service. In the course of the telephone conversation, the counsellor learned enough information to identify tentatively that the student was clinically depressed. She gave the welfare officer feedback on the significant pieces of the material, and praised her for having asked the right questions. The student felt relieved that she had made a correct referral, and also felt that now that she had discovered that she knew the right questions to ask, she would be more confident in the future.

Referrals between student unions and counselling services go both ways. Unions can be a source of practical advice and a link with social facilities, which some students may need as much as they need counselling. They can also offer a more informal and 'drop-in' service than many counselling services can provide.

The greatest difficulty in dealing with student unions is that the officers change, usually on a yearly basis. Counsellors require a great deal of energy and commitment to ensure continuity of contact with the student union. The start of the new academic year is always demanding, both of time and energy, and it can be difficult to begin again with the new union officers who occasionally, with the confidence of youth, do not themselves recognize the value of regular contact with a counselling service.

Nightline

Many universities and HE colleges, and a small number of the larger FE colleges, run a telephone helpline service for students. The helpline is usually available during term time when counselling services are closed (i.e. in the evenings, throughout the night and at weekends). It is a service run by students for students, and has the same advantages and disadvantages as welfare posts in student unions. Helplines are accessible and informal, and allow students to use their peer group for support. They also place the volunteers who run the service in extremely difficult situations for which they may require support from the counselling service. Like the Samaritans, who are often involved in the training of these helpers, most student telephone services call themselves befrienders rather than counsellors, and yet the volunteers often have to deal with immediate situations of crisis or mental breakdown. There are clearly good grounds for liaison between Nightline and counselling services. Some counselling services are asked to help with the selection of volunteers, to be involved in their training or to offer occasional supervision. But the predominant culture tends to be one where the student-run services jealously guard their independence. In doing this, they feel that they can maintain the trust of their clients. Counsellors usually respect such a stance, offer their services when required and do not intrude upon the students' territory.

Chaplaincy services

Some people argue that it is an anachronism to have chaplains in educational institutions and cannot imagine what they do. In some of the older universities, the chaplain or dean is also an academic theologian, whose main interest does not lie in the pastoral care of the students. However, most chaplains are employed, by the local diocese or church, to minister to the spiritual needs of students and to add to the resources available to students at a time of questioning and change. In the main, chaplains come from the Christian community but make it clear they are available to people of all faiths or no faith at all. A few institutions arrange for visits from clergy from other faiths, but even in an increasingly mixed cultural and religious society, the move to multi-faith chaplaincy centres has been slow. An exception is at Leicester University, where the ecumenical chaplaincy comprises Anglican, Roman Catholic, Methodist, Baptist, Congregational and Lutheran chaplains. There are also representatives from the Quakers, Unitarians and non-Christian faiths, such as Muslims, Jews and Hindus.

Few chaplains adopt a proselytizing role, although no doubt they hope that the students might see the value of a developing faith. Rather, their approach is one of being alongside students and staff. They are available to anyone who feels that they need a quiet place to ponder on the many questions provoked by being a member of an educational institution. In some ways, their work parallels that of counsellors, and indeed many have had counselling training. They also offer informal discussion groups, and enter into casual conversations with students about their day-to-day concerns regarding college or university. This raises boundary issues which can be confusing both to them and to the students. Is this a casual conversation, a request for counselling, a need for spiritual direction or even an attempt at some kind of confession? Like counsellors, chaplains are a potent vehicle for people's projections and transference material. They are very rarely allowed to be themselves and they too have to work hard to develop a realistic understanding within the institution of their role and function.

Where chaplaincies and counselling services can develop close links, there are opportunities for cross-referral and mutual support. They can often work in tandem with the same student.

A chaplain referred a student to a counselling service who had come to him for spiritual guidance. The student had expressed a wish to enter the ministry. However, in their sessions, the chaplain detected a desire in the student to set himself apart, and that this might be connected with his experience of being physically and emotionally abused as a child. Although the chaplain had counselling training, he felt that these early experiences might be more appropriately dealt with in a separate counselling setting. The counsellor and chaplain together, with the student's permission, were able, in their different ways, to help him to work through his wishes and needs.

In this particular case, the chaplain was clear that he should keep within the boundaries of spiritual guidance and encourage the student to explore the deeper psychological issues with the counsellor. At other times, the chaplain saw people for clearly contracted counselling sessions and used the counsellor as a supervisor for this work. In addition, they had worked jointly with students during the induction programme, offering informal discussions about the process of settling in. The continuity in their relationship allowed them to understand the boundaries of each other's role. It also gave them a contained space within which they could confront potential confusions in their perceptions of their respective ways of working.

MEDICAL SERVICES

In many cases, relationships between student counselling services and the medical services in the 1990s are in stark contrast with the cooperative and supportive environment created by Nicolas Malleson and his colleagues (see Chapter 1). Counselling services have developed a non-medical identity; at the same time, the NHS has undergone substantial change and many medical practitioners feel that there is little time to support anyone but themselves and their immediate patients. Both these situations have resulted in the diminution of useful contact between counselling and medical services.

The amount and quality of contact between these services depends on a number of variables: whether there is a defined student health centre with a dedicated provision; whether there is a student health centre with part-time staff who have other duties within the health services; whether there is no health centre and students are expected to register with local provision; and whether practitioners in any of these services are well disposed towards counselling.

One of the major tensions between counsellors and medical practitioners can be summed up in the phrase 'doctor knows best'. While it is important to recognize that doctors have an obligation to provide their patients with the best and most appropriate treatment, it also has to be recognized that some doctors choose to overrule or to ignore what may already be a useful relationship between a counsellor and a student.

One particular counsellor had been working for some time with a female student. The student had at first expressed panic at the beginning of her first year. She felt trapped and wanted to run away. During the course of counselling, she revealed that she had been sexually abused for a number of years by a close family friend. At one particular point when she was having to face some extremely difficult material including the fact that she was about to go home for the vacation and might see this family friend, she failed to keep two appointments. The counsellor wrote to her after each missed appointment and received no answer. About a fortnight later, the counsellor received a telephone call from the student who said she was in the local hospital, and that she felt bad that she had not been in contact. When the counselling sessions resumed on the student's return from hospital, the counsellor heard what had happened.

The student had collapsed at college. Her GP had been called and had admitted her to hospital. The incident had taken place the day before the student was due to have her counselling appointment, and she asked her GP to let her counsellor know what had happened.

Later in the week, when various tests had suggested to the hospital that there was nothing organically wrong, she was referred for psychiatric assessment. She told the psychiatrist that she was receiving regular counselling, asked him to contact her counsellor, and agreed to remain in hospital for observation. It was not until her mail was forwarded to the hospital that she realized that her counsellor had not been contacted. Although while in hospital she had desperately wanted to believe that there *was* something physically wrong with her, she had also recognized that what had happened was linked to the counselling process. She was now confused and distressed, because while she was in hospital the psychiatrist had used a confrontational model to get her to talk about her experience of being abused. After a few sessions he had said he would not be able to see her regularly but would refer her to a psychologist for long-term help. She did not know whether she should take up this referral. She had found the sessions with the psychiatrist extremely disturbing, but a part of her believed that he must know what he was doing because he was a doctor. She also saw the referral to the psychologist as an indication that the doctor felt that her regular counselling would not help.

In this case, because of his busy life, the GP may have forgotten the student's request that he should contact her counsellor. However, the student's contact with the psychiatrist was more prolonged and it seemed that he chose to ignore the student's wish that the counsellor should be informed. He also decided not to liaise with the counsellor to see if she had anything useful to contribute to the diagnosis and to possible further treatment.

A much more useful relationship between the same counsellor and another GP is illustrated in the following example:

A general practitioner contacted the counsellor to talk about one of his patients who was about to start counselling with her. He discussed with the counsellor the advisability of immediately prescribing anti-depressant medication. While the decision remained with the doctor, he wanted to take into consideration whether or not the medication might interfere with the counselling process. The counsellor and the doctor agreed to liaise, with the student's permission, and the decision about medication was delayed until it was known whether the student could manage with counselling support.

More often it is the counsellor who contacts the doctor. Counsellors sometimes need to check that there are no physical or medical reasons for a student's difficulties. At other times, they recognize the necessity for some medication if the student is to cope. This is particularly the case in the lead up to examinations when immediate anxiety, or lack of sleep, can be incapacitating. When the cycle of panic or sleeplessness has been attended to, then students are in a better position to take their examinations and perhaps also to address the psychological implications of their predicament.

Perhaps one of the reasons for not persuading doctors to take counselling seriously is that it is an unregulated activity. Although the Counselling in Medical Settings Division of BAC has published guidelines for the employment of counsellors in general practice (see East 1995), this has not countered the view that anyone, even someone with little training, can adopt the title of counsellor.

Similarly, although the accreditation criteria of ASC have helped considerably to improve the quality of student counselling, it has not stopped the appointment of untrained individuals to student counselling posts. (This issue is addressed in some detail in Chapter 6.) It remains part of the continuing tension between counsellors and other professionals, particularly those within medicine. This requires urgent attention if these allied professionals are to be persuaded that each can complement the other's practice.

Preventative and educational work

There is sometimes a need with younger students for counsellors to have contact with a sympathetic doctor or nurse who has an interest in health education and contraceptive advice. It may be that a nurse will be more immediately involved in the educational and advisory role, but the attention of a non-judgemental and careful doctor at the time of prescription can be a major advantage, and an adjunct to the counselling process as students make major life decisions. It is not true that all students leap into sexual activity without a thought for the consequences. This is refuted by the number of students who use counselling services to make serious decisions about their relationships.

Counsellors and medical services often combine to give advice on drug and alcohol misuse. In 1995, most daily newspapers reported that the majority of children have contact with drugs before they leave school. The prediction was that by the year 2000, students who had not taken drugs would be in the minority. The reality is that relatively few students consult counselling services about drug misuse, although such a problem can sometimes be identified when the initial problem of lack of concentration or depression has been explored. The reason that this is rarely presented as a problem may be because students do not actually see it as a problem. It may also be because specialist services for those with drug problems are well publicized and students go to them directly. The fact that students may not see their lack of concentration or depression as being drug-related can be a defence, but it is more likely they do not have the information to make the connection.

Because of the demands on the resources of counselling services, counsellors are less able to engage in preventative and prophylactic work than in the past. Some counsellors argue that it is not their job anyway, but the number of students whose difficulties are exacerbated by excessive alcohol consumption is of major concern. Again, students rarely see this as a primary problem, though counsellors are aware how harassment, impulsive sexual activity and an inability to work may be the result of an over-relaxed attitude to alcohol. Medical staff and counsellors need only to look at the increase in the numbers requesting the 'morning after pill' to be aware that alcohol consumption is the source of many additional problems. Whether the provision of information and advisory sessions should be the responsibility of counsellors, medical practitioners or the college or university as a whole is the subject of debate. There is even debate as to whether or not it should be provided at all – some institutions believe that by providing information regarding the effects of various drugs and alcohol, they are encouraging their use. This is an area where counsellors and medical practitioners can work in cooperation to raise the awareness of administrators and managers of institutions about the benefits of preventative work.

Psychiatric provision

Adolescents are caricatured for their apparently strange and extreme behaviour. At times they present to counselling services with florid and bizarre symptoms, and counsellors have to assess whether these are part of a passing phase or an indication of a more profound and long-lasting personality disorder. At this point, they may need the professional assessment skills of a psychiatrist who has a particular understanding of adolescence, who will not jump to immediate conclusions and who is prepared to recognize how counselling sessions can assist in the diagnostic process.

The issue of psychiatric cover has always been problematic within student counselling. Many institutions do not see it as a necessary undertaking. The idea that some students are so disturbed that they might need referral to a psychiatrist is anathema. Institutions deal with this by asserting that it is an entirely medical problem. Although FE colleges in particular have begun to admit more students who are disturbed, they have little understanding of how to support and care for such students. They seem to believe that by providing a counselling service they are attending to the problem. Counsellors are then faced with making their own contacts within the psychiatric profession.

A further difficulty is the under-provision of psychiatric and psychotherapeutic services within the NHS, and those that are available are not always appropriate to the student population. Health service provision tends to be focused on the chronically ill, who are either hospitalized or receive day care over a long period of time. The fact that students may not be resident in the hospital catchment area for a significant part of the year also calls for a different kind of provision, which hospitals are often unable, or unwilling, to provide.

It is also important to acknowledge that many psychiatrists believe that a dynamic or person-centred psychotherapeutic approach has no value. Some, as in the example quoted above, do not wish to liaise with or support counsellors in their work.

When a student is psychotic or delusional, there is normally little doubt of the need for immediate and thorough psychiatric intervention. Counsellors are relieved to find that they are not usually expected to be involved in the treatment of such students. It is rare though for students to be in such an extreme state. More often, counsellors need to check their own assessment of the severity of symptoms and to identify the appropriateness of continuing to work with disturbed students, with some background psychiatric support. It is clearly impossible to do this if the psychiatrist has no faith in the counselling approach. This is why it is important for counsellors to identify and develop good working relationships with psychiatric services personnel, who can be called upon at times of crisis and for consultation. Counsellors are fully aware that they are using resources within hard pressed health services and realize that they can only use such services at times of crisis. In these days of limited provision, some psychiatrists may also be relieved to know that a counsellor is available to see their student patients.

In order to address the need for continuous support, some counselling services now buy in the services of a psychiatric consultant for a limited number of hours each week. The psychiatrist carries out assessments on site, which means both that there is a more immediate response and that students are more likely to accept a referral. Although admissions to hospital are rare, the psychiatrist knows the system and may have access to beds. Counsellors can consult the psychiatrist without having to refer students directly and thus there is a useful monitoring of their work. The main advantage is that counsellors are able to sustain an appropriate level of work with students who otherwise might have to give up their studies in order to enter an NHS hospital. This constitutes a saving for the health services as well as for the institution, which would lose fees if the student left. To the students themselves, it is most important that they are able to carry on with their academic work and remain a student, which may itself be therapeutic. Equally, counsellors and psychiatrists can together make realistic assessments of when it is not possible for students to continue as part of the academic community. While this is again done with the students' interests in mind, it can be of advantage to the institution, especially when teachers and administrators are spending too much time and effort trying to contain a disturbed or disruptive student.

What the limitations are of an educational institution, or student counselling service, in terms of emotional, medical and psychiatric illness, are never clear. There are few absolutes, which is why the relationship between the institution, the counselling service and medical specialists should be open and consistent. Even when there are specific student health services, this dialogue can be difficult because disturbed people have a disturbing effect on the people around them. Tensions within the student may be acted out by those responsible for care. However, the proximity of these services allows for open communication. Lone counsellors, particularly those who have to liaise with a variety of GPs or with whichever psychiatrist is on duty, have a particularly difficult time. This is an area which ASC needs to address. Consideration of this and other such matters is taken up in Chapter 6.

This chapter began with liaison with tutors because they are the people with whom counsellors most often cooperate. It ends with links with medical services because these can be the most problematic. In all of these relationships, as with links with parents, social workers and home doctors, there is a clear need for a sophisticated understanding of inter-professional relationships. Many of the examples in this chapter illustrate the positive ways counsellors have found of working with allied professionals. However, these positive examples should not be taken as evidence that this work is easy or straightforward. It is frequently the source of frustration, disappointment and conflict. But where such relationships are good, this is usually the result of painstaking contact over a long period of time. Another factor in working effectively with others and ensuring support in times of difficulty is an understanding of organizational dynamics: the need for counsellors working in educational institutions to be trained in this area is one of the issues discussed in the final chapter.

· SIX ·

A critique of counselling in further and higher education

Many of the hopes of the pioneers of student counselling have been realized. Yet, paradoxically, there is a general feeling in student counselling of insecurity and vulnerability. This is due mainly to the major changes in funding arrangements in both further and higher education. Institutions themselves are also feeling vulnerable. They have to be seen to be functioning as businesses, with much of their time taken up considering which aspects of their operations are profitable. They are also forced to cut those services which appear to be a drain on resources. Counselling services are often having to justify their existence in a more forthright way, thus resurrecting many of the questions addressed at the beginning of the development of student counselling, including what constitutes counselling (or perhaps more specifically, competent counselling), what makes for a good counselling service, and whether an institution should have a counselling service at all.

WHAT IS COUNSELLING?

Throughout this book it has been acknowledged that there are many individuals in educational institutions who employ counselling skills. In many ways, they are 'front-line' practitioners who deserve to be included in this book. However, the question that needs to be addressed in a clear and uncompromising way is, what is a counsellor?

It may seem to be tautological to pose this question when there are so many people designated counsellors in the educational field. The question has been addressed, at length, in a variety of ways. There is a definition contained in BAC literature, accreditation schemes have been developed both by ASC and BAC, and the Differentiation Project has helped to define the commonalities and the differences between befriending, advice, guidance and counselling. However, despite these definitions, there is, in practice, considerable obfuscation.

This is due partly to the expressed intention since the founding of ASC, that the Association should be inclusive rather than exclusive. This has been both its strength and its weakness. Its strength has been in the way that it has encouraged those whose interest is counselling, and it has set standards to which they should aspire. It has also recognized and valued the contribution of those who employ counselling skills but who do not see themselves as counsellors. More pragmatically, the larger membership has produced the finance that has allowed specific developments to take place which have contributed to the acceptance of student counselling as a professional activity. The weakness has been that, despite the increased value placed on accreditation, the scheme is still seen only as a means to encourage higher standards. It is never described overtly as the minimum standard for good practice. In Chapter 1, it was noted that most advertisements for bona fide student counselling posts require applicants to have ASC accreditation. This demonstrates the influence that ASC has had in encouraging institutions to take these posts seriously. However, there are still a number of people practising student counselling in addition to other duties (where the 'post' has never been formalized), and others who have moved into posts incrementally, where ASC has been unable to influence the process of appointment. Often those who occupy these posts are not trained to the level of ASC accreditation. ASC does not say that people who are not fully trained should not be practising.

Many would argue that this is no different from counselling as a whole and would point to present-day experienced practitioners who have developed their counselling skills by 'learning on the job'. The proposed National Vocational Qualifications support the idea that competency can be achieved through experience in the workplace. However, the various elements of competency that are grouped together to constitute a qualification within the NVQ system set out a minimum level of competency acceptable to the field. ASC has contributed to the development of these qualifications and thus has been able to say what makes a competent counsellor. The question of whether ASC could, or would wish to, convince employing institutions that counsellors should not be employed unless they meet these criteria remains unanswered.

A further challenge to the inclusive nature of ASC is the

development of the UK Register of Counsellors. The agreed criteria state that there are two routes to registration: as an independent practitioner or through sponsorship by an organization. The underpinning rationale for the register is that both routes provide an assurance of safety and accountability for clients. The route for independent practitioners, through the accreditation schemes of BAC or the Confederation of Scottish Counselling Agencies (COSCA), assumes a level of training, experience and supervision that will allow practitioners to work safely without management supervision. The route through sponsoring organizations allows counsellors, who sometimes will have less experience and training, to be registered to counsel within that specific organization. The organization takes responsibility for ensuring the quality and safety of their practitioners' work, demonstrates a commitment to the professional development of the counsellors they sponsor, and must have a code of ethics and practice and a complaints procedure in place. If the scheme is as effective as the originators hope, then within the immediate future the public, including employers, will become aware that registration indicates an appropriate level of safety and quality.

Many student counsellors will be eligible to apply for registration as independent practitioners. As experienced counsellors they can demonstrate that they are capable of working autonomously, although many of them have chosen to work in well-developed teams. The dilemma for ASC is that a number of lone counsellors will not be eligible to apply for independent registration. Neither will they be able to be registered through a sponsoring organization, since the criteria state that a sponsoring organization should have responsibility for not less than three people. It can also be argued that lone counsellors take as much responsibility for casework as independent practitioners who work in private practice: there is no-one to refer to on a daily basis; their work is not supervised in a management sense; they have to be able to identify their own needs for professional development; and they must be able to assess if a client needs medical or psychiatric help. This line of argument would suggest that all lone counsellors must be of independent practitioner status.

If ASC wishes to continue to support those who are committed to counselling but have not yet reached the required standard for BAC or COSCA accreditation, and thus independent practitioner status, it may have to consider taking responsibility for their work by becoming a sponsoring organization itself. This would require a major shift in the structure and practice of the Association that would be both financially and administratively difficult. It is possible for very small organizations to form a consortium and take on the role of a sponsoring organization. However, even if lone counsellors avail themselves of this route, they still have to demonstrate that the consortium meets the requirements for a sponsoring organization. A consortium of less experienced practitioners would be unlikely to meet these requirements. If ASC cannot, or does not wish to, take on the role of a sponsoring organization, then these lone, inexperienced practitioners will not be registered.

The development of the UK Register of Counsellors challenges counselling as a whole to define and regulate itself and ASC will have to make its position clear. If it gives validity to practitioners who are unregistered, it will compromise its position as the arbiter of standards in student counselling. If it cannot find a way of continuing to value and support embryonic student counsellors, it will be seen to reject a large number of its members. The tension at the founding meeting of ASC between those who wanted the Association to be for 'professional' counsellors only and those who wanted the Association to be all-embracing can again be felt. However, twenty-five years later it cannot be resolved by a creative fudging of the issues. ASC will have to declare what is, and what is not, an appropriate level of training, experience and competence for those who wish to call themselves student counsellors.

This not only has implications for the Association's own structures, but it challenges the way that counselling has developed in many institutions. It could be argued that this is an inappropriate time to be making such a challenge, that it is better to have a little counselling in some institutions than no counselling at all. That registered counsellors will be seen to be too expensive is all too readily apparent. The quality assurance criteria of the Higher and Further Education Funding Councils state that each institution must indicate the facilities available for guidance and personal counselling. This is also repeated in the Students' Charter. However, what would at first appear to be a strong position from which counsellors can negotiate also has hidden hazards. In the further education document in particular there is some indication that counselling is understood to mean help with financial and accommodation problems. If this is all the institutions are instructed to provide, then, it is argued, colleges will not be prepared to fund counselling as defined by ASC. Some colleges have already decided that they can meet the funding criteria by devolving the 'counselling' component to youth workers and welfare workers who are cheaper to employ. Within this climate, there are many members of ASC who fear that by drawing attention to the need for registered counsellors, counselling as they understand it will disappear from many FE colleges.

This disparity between what counsellors and their institutions perceive counselling to be is not confined to FE colleges. Throughout education as a whole there are misunderstandings about what goes on in the counselling room. Many institutions assume that the counselling they fund is fundamentally problem-solving in nature. They have little understanding of the deeply therapeutic work that is often also necessary in order for students to take full advantage of educational opportunities. As Ellen Noonan clearly defines it:

> Nearly everyone who comes to see us brings a reality problem to be sorted out and an unconscious to be explored, an anxiety to be relieved and a phantasy to be untangled, an acute need to be helped and a transference relationship to be tested out.
>
> (Noonan 1983: ix)

Many counsellors use their annual report to describe the complexities of the counselling relationship. It is one way of publicizing their work to the maximum number of people. It also means that if the report is accepted, they have at the very least an indirect mandate to carry on with the work they describe.

In 1993, four well-regarded counselling services each advertised a full-time counselling post. None felt able to appoint from the considerable number of applicants. Each of the heads of service was troubled by this and began to question whether they were too demanding in their requirements. It was when the four came together at a meeting and by chance began to discuss their non-appointments that they discovered that there were a number of common features in their decisions not to appoint. Each had found that few of the applicants were able to describe their work in a way that was understandable to the academic members of staff on the interviewing committee. One academic observed, 'I could describe counselling better than any of these'. Another problem was the number of highly trained counsellors and psychotherapists who seemed to want to operate as private practitioners within the institution. The appointment panels felt that their inability to see their responsibility to the institution as well as to the client would render them incapable of coping with the *Sturm und Drang* of life as a counsellor in education. Others had little concept of how the institution itself might impact on the therapeutic work with the client. It is important to note that the four heads of service were representative of the major theoretical schools, but all agreed that to appoint people who could not describe their work clearly, or who were unprepared for the realities of counselling in an institution, would undermine the definition, understanding and acceptance of counselling in their particular organizations. This seems to paint a very gloomy picture of the quality of people applying for jobs as student counsellors. It can also be seen as an indication that student counselling requires specific skills and understanding and experienced practitioners who are sure of who they are and what they do.

Training courses and trainees

One way to ensure that there are sufficiently trained practitioners is to influence training courses. ASC's (1993) *Guide to Training Courses in Counselling* sets out essential and desirable features in the training of potential student counsellors. If these are adhered to, then those completing their training should be capable of working within an educational context. However, not all courses meet these requirements, and there is a need for experienced counsellors to provide feedback on these courses and explain the specific needs of the profession of student counselling.

Very few courses require counsellors to be trained to work therapeutically in the short term. This is a very difficult issue to address, since it is generally believed that it is not possible for counsellors to undertake short-term therapy unless they have a thorough understanding and experience of working long term. A different view, however, is held at the University of Warwick, where it is proposed to offer a training in short-term therapy. The intention is that its graduates will be qualified in short-term therapy only (i.e. they will not be qualified to work with long-term clients). While this proposed course will add to the debate about short-term work, because of its specific focus it will not equip people to work in student counselling: student counsellors need to be able to work with some clients over a long period of time. These two extremes, the large number of courses that do not address short-term work at all and the proposed course that will address short-term work only, illustrate the difficulty producing adequately trained student counsellors.

If there are difficulties matching training to individual client work in student counselling, it is even more difficult to locate courses that provide enough attention to the complexities of working in organizational settings. Some courses invite other professionals to teach on the course. Others offer insight into the work of other professionals by having a series of one-off lectures. In this way, students begin to learn to work inter-professionally. However, it is very rare for such courses to study, in depth, how counselling and counsellors are affected by working inside an organization. Student counsellors need to understand how systems work and what can both enhance and inhibit their professional work. They need this understanding because it can be evident when clients unconsciously take on the anxieties of the institution. They need to understand how the framework of the organization influences their practice, and they need to understand how to work within the system – how boundaries can be maintained while developing a flexible and open organization within a larger organization. Without this they will not be fully equipped to practise.

Most courses insist that students have training placements and most established student counselling services are regularly approached to provide placement opportunities. When such placements are an integral part of the course, it is easier for the service to be sure that the student will be capable of working in that specific setting and that the setting will contribute to the student's development. However, many courses have no contact with the placement setting and are concerned only that the student gains experience somewhere and that he or she will have case material to discuss on the course. These are not real placements, but merely an insistence that students have some experience of counselling during their training. Since some counselling experience is a prerequisite of the course, some people become extremely discouraged when they are told that because of the range and complexity of the problems presented, they cannot start practising as a student counsellor until they have had some formal training. However, placements can be provided when the student has completed a substantial part of the course. This is perhaps one of the most useful ways that student counsellors have of influencing the content of training. If a spread of long-, medium- and short-term work is provided and attention is paid to the experience of working in an institution, students begin to have a real understanding of the work. If there is, in addition, a formal dialogue with the training course, organizers of courses can be briefed and the curriculum amended where necessary.

The European dimension

The latest challenge to the definition of counselling in Britain has come from mainland Europe. It comes from counselling and psychotherapy as a whole and from the particular context of student counselling.

In Chapter 2, brief reference was made to the difficulties encountered with the concepts of advice, guidance and counselling in the English language. In other European countries where there is only one word for the three activities, it is even more difficult to translate the British concept of counselling. It was in the European context that the term 'therapeutic counselling' (see Chapter 2) was first used in an attempt to describe the function of the work of British counsellors. In the European student counselling field, the term 'psychological counselling' is also used. A further complication is that the accepted definition of psychotherapy in Britain is periodically challenged by regulations in other countries and by those who are determined to restrict the title of psychotherapist to those with qualifications in medicine or psychology. These groups do not recognize counselling as having any relation or relevance to their activity as psychotherapists.

Those who practise what would be recognizable as student counselling in Britain must be trained as a psychologist in every other European country apart from Britain and Ireland. Most have an additional qualification in psychotherapy. When the Psychological Counselling in Higher Education (PSYCHE) group (Bell *et al.* 1994) first began its cross-European work, there was considerable dismay that British and Irish practitioners were engaged in this work without a first degree in psychology. During the six years the members have worked together, they have learned to understand and appreciate each other's work. There is no discernible differences in the quality of the therapeutic work between those who have had a psychology training and those who have not. But despite the fact that mainland European practitioners value the contribution of their British and Irish colleagues, when they were invited to join the new European Association for Counselling a number declined. They said openly that it would be politically unwise for them to be seen by their country to be allying themselves with counselling.

At the present time there is a cordial co-existence between student counsellors and psychologists in the various European countries and they are eager to learn from each other's work. The signs are that this will improve in the future. But the broader context of counselling and psychotherapy means that student counsellors in Britain may need to take great care that their profession and qualifications are recognized. The experience of those working in higher education is that there is no difference in the function, despite the difference in training and title between student counsellors, psychologists and psychotherapists. Although it is unlikely that the European Commission will produce a directive in the immediate

future, student counsellors need to be aware that the lobby to
do so is strong. This is why it is important that the profession of
student counselling takes the issue of registration and government
recognition seriously.

A GOOD COUNSELLING SERVICE?

There are two aspects to the question of what makes a good counselling service: the first relates to provision and the second to quality of delivery. Quantity cannot ensure quality, but the delivery of
a quality service may well depend on the resources available.

Resources

An interesting example of the pressure student counsellors are under
in the 1990s surfaced while gathering information for this book.
Counsellors who are widely felt to be offering a good service did not
want to be quoted in case their resources were cut. Those who felt
the provision was poor did not want to be named in case it made
things worse. The fear that attention will be drawn to a particular
service inevitably makes it difficult for standards to be set and for
an argument to be made for equality of provision. This disparity in
provision is best illustrated by three examples of funding in 1995.

One university student counselling service, while reasonably well
resourced compared with many others, is still subject to waiting lists
from time to time and is under pressure to find more efficient ways
of working. However, for three years it has been the subject of a
special fund promoted by the vice-chancellor at the time of his annual
oration. This has brought the counselling service approximately
£7000 in extra income each year.

A second university has always valued and supported its counselling service. The staff of the service have been prominent in the
development of student counselling and have shown political as-
tuteness in relation to their own organization. In 1995, the counselling service's budget was cut by £10,000. It could be argued that
the service was treated no differently from any other department in
the university at a time of financial pressure. However, the impact
on this small service in a large institution is considerable. The service is able to present evidence that at certain times of the year it
is impossible to keep pace with demand, yet in order to maintain
staffing levels it will have to generate income. In order to generate
the missing £10,000, counsellors will have to reduce client contact

time, inevitably increasing waiting time for counselling and adding to student pressure.

Finally, an FE college has decided to close down its in-house counselling service completely. It does not accept that it should provide therapeutic counselling and has decided to concentrate its resources on guidance and advice.

Even when institutions are well disposed towards counselling, the fear is often openly expressed that they are pouring money into a 'black hole'. They suspect that there is an insatiable demand, and that demand will always outstrip supply. In contrast with this pessimistic view, many of the British delegates at the European vice-chancellors' conference in Barcelona were eager to know what they *should* provide. They admitted that they might not be able to meet the requirements in full – few university departments have everything that they need. However, the British delegates wanted to know what their targets should be. ASC, through its advisory service to institutions, has stated that there should be one counsellor to every 2000 students. However, this ratio is seen by many institutions as being based on opinion rather than on analysis. If ASC is to capitalize on the goodwill of these vice-chancellors and others like them, it needs to make clear how it has arrived at its recommendations.

The provision of an appropriate number of counsellors is only one of the indicators of an adequately resourced service. As ASC has maintained from its inception, there needs to be accommodation that is safe, welcoming and private; counsellors' salaries need to be in line with posts of equal responsibility in the institution; there must be an opportunity and space for reflection on their work; time must be allowed for appropriate administration; and counsellors must have access to supervision.

Many services use the BAC Codes of Ethics and Practice as a lever to insist on supervision arrangements. However, this insistence on working to a code drawn up outside the institution can be seen by the college or university as a threat rather than a support to good practice. One vice-chancellor referred to it as 'trades union restrictive practice'. It may well be the case in the future, as educational organizations scrutinize every aspect of their budgets, that it will not be enough for counsellors simply to state that supervision arrangements *must* be in place. They will have to make clear *why* they should be in place. Institutions need to be persuaded that it is in their interests for counsellors to be externally supervised. It is an expensive provision and a convincing case needs to be made.

An equally difficult subject in relation to resources is the provision of good reception and secretarial staff. In many small institutions, such support does not exist. The counsellors in these institutions have devised ways of arranging appointments in a safe and confidential way, for example by having an appointment sheet attached to the door showing pre-booked sessions with no names attached. New students fill in the word 'booked', or their initials, against an available slot. The main problem with this system is that if there are no slots available and the counsellor is engaged all day, no-one is available to assess the urgency of any new clients. Some counsellors who work within this system keep a few slots each day for 'walk-in' appointments. This gives them the chance to deal with brief inquiries, and allows students who have an urgent need to make contact. This, too, can create as many problems as it appears to solve. There is no way of knowing how many students will 'walk in' and how much time they are going to need during the initial contact. Counsellors need to be extraordinarily disciplined in how they conduct these sessions if they are to remain accessible; and even the best organized and disciplined counsellors may find that their carefully defined boundaries have to be redefined in the face of student distress.

It seems unlikely in institutions where heads of academic departments have inadequate secretarial support that dedicated provision will be made for counsellors, however convincing the case. In these institutions, it is doubly important that counsellors are aware of the impact of the structure of the institution on their therapeutic work, and that they find a way of communicating to their colleagues the limitations of what their service can provide. In many cases, colleagues will be supportive if they are convinced that attempts are being made to manage limited resources well. They become angry, suspicious and unsupportive if they do not understand why things are being managed in the way they are.

In some larger institutions, the reception and secretarial support is shared with other members of student services. This has obvious financial advantages and can contribute to the sense of an integrated student service provision. Those who support this system point out that it depathologizes counselling – it is presented as just one more service among many others. However, it is often underestimated how difficult it is for students to feel that their privacy is respected if they have to make a counselling appointment in the middle of a busy office. In addition, the particular skills and understanding required of receptionists of counselling services might not be acknowledged within this system of broad provision.

Those who are fortunate enough to work in a service where

there is good secretarial and receptionist support appreciate how important such staff are to the service. It is not just that good secretaries keep the administration running smoothly, but that they take on many tasks that release counsellors to counsel. As well as dealing with the appointment system, correspondence and telephone calls, they collate data on the use of the service and prepare this for statistical and reporting purposes. Many also deal with day-to-day budgeting aspects and attend to the 'domestic' arrangements of the service. Far from being a luxury, they are essential if counselling resources are to be used cost-effectively. Most importantly, they make sure that students are received well when they arrive at the service.

Receptionists are the public face of the counselling service, often dealing with students at their most distressed. They need to know how to listen, what questions to ask, and how to contain anxiety. They also need to know if students are showing signs of being at risk. Many counsellors rely on and trust their receptionists' judgement as to whether an extra space needs to be created in an already crowded diary to deal with a particularly urgent case. Pat Bizley, when she was senior counsellor at the then Leicester Polytechnic, ran an annual training course for receptionists of counselling services in further and higher education in recognition of the particular skills required, and a number of services encourage their receptionists to undergo basic counselling training.

There is no general agreement about whether or not receptionists and secretaries should attend weekly counselling service meetings. They usually attend the administrative part of the meeting but are asked to leave before case discussions begin. Other services believe that secretaries and receptionists are part of the 'circle of confidentiality' offered by the service and include them in every aspect of team discussion. They find that secretaries and receptionists value this involvement and the work of the service benefits because they are better able to contain their own and others' anxiety when they understand how counsellors work. However the work of secretaries and receptionists is incorporated into the work of the service as a whole, it is generally recognized that they bring their own professionalism to the service and that their contribution is essential to the delivery of a good service.

Service delivery

Views on what constitutes good service delivery depends upon the perspective of the assessor. These differing perspectives can produce tension and, occasionally, conflict. An institution might want its counselling service to see as many people as possible for as short a time as possible. The counselling service, on the other hand, might prefer not to make students feel they are under pressure to resolve things prematurely. Students might express a need for answers in a few sessions, while counsellors might think that the process of change needs time. ASC wants its members to work developmentally and preventatively, whereas some institutions want their counsellors to stay in their counselling rooms. Perhaps the only thing that a manager of a counselling service can be sure of is that the service will never meet everyone's expectations.

One problem institutions have when assessing how well a counselling service is functioning, is that they do not know what questions to ask. They might even feel that they should not be asking questions at all, because the work of a counselling service is, by definition, confidential. In order to address this, ASC has published a *Guide to Recognizing Best Practice* (Bell *et al.* undated). Managers who are not counsellors are offered a series of questions, with possible answers, that they might reasonably ask of a service. The authors suggest that if the service can demonstrate that it thinks about and monitors its work appropriately, then managers can be assured that they have a good service.

While the aim of this publication is to state clearly to managers that student counselling can and should be accountable, it has a parallel function for counsellors themselves. It offers a template for counsellors to assess their own work and to begin to compare their service with others. Perhaps most importantly for counsellors, the authors represent the predominant theoretical models in student counselling and have reached agreement on a paradigm of good service delivery.

An extension to this work has been prompted by the developing processes of quality assurance in higher education. One of the criteria in the quality assurance documents is that the faculty being assessed should indicate facilities for student support. The result of this is that each time a different faculty is assessed in an institution, the assessors are directed to the counselling service. Occasionally, this is a paper exercise, but most frequently the assessor visits the service. Since there are many faculties in universities, counselling services receive many visits! It has been the experience of most counsellors that the assessors are reluctant to ask questions because of their perception of the counsellors' position on confidentiality. In order to address this, the Heads of University Counselling Services group has agreed with the Committee of Vice-Chancellors and

College Principals (CVCP) that benchmark standards should be drawn up. This will give examples of good practice across the whole range of service provision. With the added benefit of the imprimatur of the CVCP, this publication will be a major influence.

However welcome and timely this publication may be, it does not set out to say what each service *should* provide. In fact, it takes great care to stress in its introduction that each service will be influenced by its setting and by the predisposition of individual counsellors. It also states that there should be an acknowledgement of the diversity of provision. There is no suggestion that services should conform to a blueprint. Flexibility to match provision to setting is essential, but there is still a need for minimum standards of provision and quality. Without them institutions will not know what they must provide and what they can expect of their counselling service. Equally it leaves services vulnerable to the changing whim of managers and administrators. This is illustrated by developments at Stirling University in 1994. After the resignation of its two part-time counsellors, the university decided that there was no need for an in-house counselling service. It proposed to have someone available to whom students could make a request for counselling. This individual (not a counsellor) was to make an assessment of whether or not the student needed counselling and refer to agencies outside the university. Prompted by the adverse publicity, a senior administrator wrote to other universities in Britain asking for details of their counselling provision. The university then stated that provision across universities was so disparate that no conclusion could be drawn as to what basic provision should be. The message was that they had not been persuaded that what the university proposed was inadequate.

A more complicated mixture of views on what constitutes a good counselling service was demonstrated at Cambridge University. Service provision was commented upon favourably in a report by quality assessors. They also drew attention to the complicated financial and management structure that the service worked under, partly funded by the central administration of the university and partly by colleges. The review had discerned that this led to complexities in accountability and produced tensions. The vice-chancellor subsequently set up and chaired a committee to review the work and structure of the counselling service. It was understood that he had done this with the intent of addressing a long-standing difficulty and the counselling service welcomed the review.

The results of the two-year review was reported by the Director of the service to the Heads of University Counselling Services group, who viewed the results with increasing concern. It is important to stress that the review committee was, in the main, supportive of the service's work and recommended increased staffing and a revised management structure. The concern for the members of the Cambridge service, and for other heads of service, was the range of views about what was a satisfactory service.

The most important area of conflict was in the basic funding arrangements. Some years previously, the service had reluctantly agreed to a system of core funding whereby students could have up to sixteen sessions of counselling. If students needed more than this, the service had to approach the student's college for extra funding. This system had proved problematic to manage and implement, not least because of issues of confidentiality. While some colleges were prepared to pay for extra sessions without any argument, others insisted that a name had to be given to the college. Others refused to pay at all. A disproportionate amount of time was taken up in negotiation with colleges for this extra funding. It was an inefficient system and the director deemed that the extra costs outweighed the benefits.

In order to produce the extra funding to implement the review committee's recommendation for extra staffing, it was proposed that the core funding should cover ten sessions only per client. The counselling service was adamant that this would make good practice impossible. They felt they had a responsibility and an ethical duty to offer a confidential service. The colleges were equally adamant that they had a duty to make sure their money was being spent appropriately. The view was also expressed that the colleges had a responsibility for their students and that they should be told if a student needed longer-term counselling. The funding arrangements allowed conflicting views to surface regarding who should make decisions about what students might need.

Another area of conflict was illustrated by the clinical audit commissioned by the review committee and carried out by members of the local health service audit team. The report revealed a high number of severely depressed and disturbed people using the counselling service. This was something the counsellors had claimed for a long time and they were pleased that an independent review had confirmed their findings. The conflict was in the audit team's recommendation as to how this should be addressed. They stated that counselling was of use to people with circumscribed problems that could be resolved in a few sessions. They therefore recommended that if students were not seen to improve after four sessions, they should be referred to their GP who would decide on the need for medication or referral to a NHS psychologist. A further recommendation was that the service should employ a full-time psychologist who would be in a position to monitor counsellors' assessments. The audit team's assessment of what constituted good counselling was not one that would have been shared by any other university counselling service in the country.

The students also had a view. They felt that they were not being heard and they therefore resorted to the press. They wanted more resources for the service; they stressed the need for absolute confidentiality; they said they trusted the service and knew it to be good, but were concerned about the length of the waiting list at certain times of the year. They wanted a service they could be confident would see students when they needed it and for as long as they needed it.

The review committee sought the views of other professionals. Many said that they deemed the service to be working appropriately. Others said that the service should change its theoretical orientation; that is, if it were less psychodynamically oriented and took a more cognitive approach, then its problems would be resolved. The review committee surveyed other counselling services and reported the Cambridge service was just above the average in terms of sessions spent with clients, but that this could be explained by the specific population and the high numbers of disturbed people using the service as confirmed by the clinical audit. This did not stop one senior tutor declaring to the local press that the service was inefficient and ineffective. It seemed that everyone had a view on what counselling should be and how a counselling service should function. Few of them were prepared to listen to the counsellors.

This case demonstrates how vulnerable services are if there are no nationally agreed criteria. To most student counsellors, the Cambridge service operated well. Although not party to information about the precise management and administrative functioning of the service, they were aware that the service provided paralleled their own. If a student counselling service with experienced and respected counsellors could be so damagingly and publicly criticized by those with no knowledge of counselling, then all services were vulnerable.

Preventative and developmental work

This kind of work is seen by ASC as an essential component of good service delivery. But some of the difficulties inherent in this work need to be described and analysed if the Association is to be sure that the work is being carried out appropriately. The problem is that it is *very* difficult work and needs considerable experience if it is to be carried out effectively. In addition, counsellors are only able to carry out this work if they have gained the trust of their academic colleagues. Too many counsellors present themselves as consultants to the university or college as a whole before they have established their credibility as practising counsellors.

Some counsellors feel that they must change the ethos of the whole institution or else they are failing as student counsellors. They resort to finding places to exert their influence, which are not necessarily appropriate to the role. There is a place for counsellors on, for example, committees related to disablement and harassment. They can bring a perspective not found in other parts of the institution, based on an understanding of the psychological aspects of such issues. However, some counsellors step outside their role and become *the* campaigner on behalf of others in the institution. They need to ask themselves whether they are serving counselling well by doing this. In one college, a student in his early counselling sessions displayed overt racial prejudice. When he had learned to trust the counsellor, he was able to see that this was based on his own feelings of inferiority. It is unlikely that this student would have approached the service if the counsellor was known to chair the harassment panel of the college.

The area of study skills presents a much more subtle difficulty for counsellors in deciding what is an appropriate level of involvement. Mary Swainson (see Chapter 1) was one of the first, during the development of student counselling, to bring a psychoanalytic perspective to study skills. Her example has been followed by many counsellors and there is now a body of knowledge and experience within the profession for which many students have been grateful. However, Swainson began this work when she was still a lecturer. She had not at this point taken up a formal counselling role. Her insights were incorporated into her teaching. This highlights a question that student counsellors need to ask of themselves: Who should be *teaching* study skills? Many counsellors come from a teaching background and those with a psychology training have studied learning theory. It seems natural and appropriate that they would want to incorporate their understanding of how people learn into the range of provision offered by their services. However, a number of services appear to have taken on a teaching role when perhaps they would be better teaching the teachers. In one college, a counsellor gave an in-service seminar for teaching staff on teaching study skills. At the end of the seminar, she was asked by a senior academic if she would give a series of workshops to students in his department. She declined but suggested that she would do the workshops if he would do them with her. She pointed out to the lecturer that there was a dangerous message to the students if she did the workshops on her own. The students might hear that the department was interested in *what* they learned but only the counselling service was interested in *how* they learned. The lecturer agreed and for the next two years both the counsellor and he worked on a six-week programme. By the third year he was running the sessions on his own.

In many institutions, academics refer immediately to a counselling service when a student expresses a study difficulty. A number of academics, particularly in the university sector, have had no formal training in how to teach. In addition, those who have been successful students themselves find it difficult to identify their own study techniques and pass them on to others, since they have never had to think about them. However, student counsellors need to ask themselves whether it is appropriate for a student to be referred to them because he or she has difficulty with structuring an essay. By taking on this task for their colleagues and the institution, they absolve the institution of the responsibility of teaching students how to learn. Only if there have been a number of attempts to teach the student how to write an essay and there is still no improvement is a referral to a counselling service an appropriate response. Where there is an emotional or psychological reason why learning cannot take place, this *is* the province of a counselling service.

Serving on committees and dealing with study difficulties are important functions of a good counselling service. But sometimes engaging in these activities is an unhealthy way of counsellors making sure that their service is in demand. The skill in developmental work is to sow seeds and facilitate their growth, rather than taking on responsibility for the design and management of the entire garden.

WHY HAVE A COUNSELLING SERVICE?

Every day counsellors see how counselling makes it possible for some students to take greater advantage of education and in many cases complete their studies. While counselling may not yet be indispensable, they know that they contribute in an important way to the life of their institution.

Those who question the value of counselling services to educational institutions do not necessarily question the value of counselling itself. Administrators want to know why *they* should be providing it and what benefit it is to *them*. One administrator asked why his college should provide a private mental health service. This question illustrates the perception that counselling services are wholly private affairs, detached from the central work of the institution. In many ways, good counselling services offer what can be described as the best kind of occupational mental health service, rather than a private service offered as an add-on, occupational perk.

In 1994, Nottingham University increased its counselling service by two full-time staff. The new counsellors were appointed so that the service could deal specifically with staff. In doing this, the university was bringing itself into line with much of industry, where there has been a marked increase in the level of counselling provision. It would be foolish to imagine that large commercial organizations have introduced counselling simply out of altruism. There is self-interest. They know it reduces absenteeism, engenders a feeling in staff of being looked after and therefore makes them more committed – ultimately, it increases productivity. They may also be motivated by some anxiety produced by a case of a social worker in Northumberland who successfully took his employers to court claiming that he was subjected to unnecessary stress in the workplace. The court ruled that employers had a responsibility to monitor the emotional well-being of staff in relation to their work.

Students' work is to study. If their psychological or emotional state is such that they cannot think, then they cannot work. The 'employers', the university or the college, have a responsibility to their students to ensure that they are fit for work. They have also a financial responsibility to make sure that the institution as a whole remains productive. The fact that funding is now based on the numbers of students who complete courses, rather than on the number who joined them, may prompt them to view their counselling services in a new light.

There are some students for whom it is entirely appropriate that they leave college or university. It would be most inappropriate for counselling services to ally themselves so completely with the institution that counsellors feel they cannot help students to reach the healthy conclusion to leave. However, most students who contemplate leaving do not really want to do so. They simply find that they cannot cope with conflicting demands. When there seems to be an intractable problem at home, or when a long-held emotional problem becomes overwhelming, the tendency is to look for what can be changed, and where pressure can be released. Often students take a premature decision, as if their only option is to release themselves from the pressure of academic life. It is the one aspect of their lives over which they feel they have some control.

Rickinson and Rutherford (1995) show the influence of the counselling service at Birmingham University in increasing undergraduate retention rates. A questionnaire was designed and administered to all first-year students in the seventh week of the first term. Undergraduates who had withdrawn in the first term were also surveyed. There was a 33.3 per cent response rate. The aims of the study were:

(1) To identify factors which influence withdrawal/retention rates in the first term.
(2) To explore the hypothesis that counselling intervention can increase retention rates in the first term.
(3) To increase understanding of how student commitment can be fostered.

(Rickinson and Rutherford 1995: 163)

The respondents still at university were assessed as being of low, medium or high risk of leaving. Sixteen students in the high-risk group indicated in the space provided on the questionnaire that they wished to be contacted by the counselling service. They were offered an initial counselling session, the possibility of liaison with their personal tutor, an opportunity to attend the 'introductory workshop programme' provided by the service, and an individual review session with a counsellor with the possibility of further counselling if required. One of the students left university before the initial appointment, but the other fifteen were shown to benefit from the counselling intervention and successfully completed their first year.

Although this research reveals that the transition to university has a personal meaning for each individual student, there are common factors that indicate what a university might do to provide support. It highlights the fact that none of the students who had sought help from the counselling service had been able to use the other forms of help available in the institution. The report states: 'It appeared that their normal coping mechanisms of seeking appropriate help had been undermined by the level of their anxiety and distress'. The active intervention of the counselling service, in the form of the questionnaire, allowed them to marshal their personal resources enough for them to be able to ask for help.

This report illustrates how counselling services can alert institutions to general difficulties and is an appropriate way of working preventatively and developmentally. It shows how intervention by the counselling service can help both the institution and individual students to achieve their aims. It demonstrates that a properly resourced service that is allowed to enter into and comment on the academic life of the institution can contribute to the institution's objectives – so that it is not a private mental health service but a service in tune with and responding to the institution it seeks to serve. Some counsellors find it difficult to engage with the concept of assisting their institution to be 'productive'. The language and the ethos of the business world feels challenging to all that counsellors hold dear. The same feelings were aroused when the language of performance indicators were introduced into education some years ago. There is no doubt that counselling involves a great deal that cannot be measured in obvious terms, but it is a harsh fact that counselling services will not survive if they cannot be seen to contribute to the mainstream objectives of a university or college. More research is needed, like the Birmingham research, that demonstrates that it is possible to take on the language of the marketplace, but to do so with integrity.

Research also needs to be published in order for it to have credibility; this is what academics expect. While the need for published research is important throughout student counselling, this is particularly the case in further education, where very little has been written about services and what they provide. Much of what is published about student counselling comes from North America and is not immediately applicable within the British system. Researchers there have shown that it is possible to identify and assess those aspects of student counselling that contribute to the development of education. The increase in the number of Masters degrees in counselling in Britain has allowed for the beginnings of a research base here too, but unless it is published it remains largely inaccessible to those who need to prove to their institutions that a counselling service is a vital part of provision.

CONCLUSION

Many of the questions posed in this chapter have had to be faced by individual counsellors in their own institutions. They have been supported in this by the work of ASC and its various publications. ASC itself has managed to influence, to an extraordinary degree, the development of the whole of student counselling. And yet the profession of student counselling is still vulnerable. Some argue that this is because the climate in education is so hostile to everything that counselling stands for, that nobody really wants to know. It is therefore not the fault of counselling that it is not accepted without question: the reality of the situation must be taken on board and acknowledged. There are, indeed, many factors – both conscious and unconscious – that govern the acceptance of counselling in education. It is very difficult to admit to problems, not least in students, when everyone is being pressed to show how successful and competitive they are. Faced with this, some counsellors – who also operate at both a conscious and unconscious level – begin to blame themselves rather than blame the external climate: 'It's our fault; we're not professional enough; we can't sell ourselves and make a convincing case for what we do'. Attaching blame to the external environment may bring immediate relief; blaming oneself may be a way of avoiding confronting the situation in the outside world; but neither position brings lasting relief nor does it promote a creative solution.

The reality is that even in these days of cost-cutting, individual entrepreneurialism and a preoccupation with corporate goals, there are many people in education who share the values on which counselling is based. The challenge for counsellors and for ASC is to locate these people and to work out what can be done jointly to ensure that their shared values are preserved.

One of the most outstanding features in the early development of student counselling (see Chapter 1) was the way in which the pioneers recognized that their cause could be strengthened by working collaboratively with those who had more influence than themselves. They did not indulge in grandiose ideas that they alone were responsible for the development of student counselling. The situation they faced then remains the same today. However good a service is, it will always remain a tiny part of a large institution and have minimal influence on the politics of the organization. The same is true of ASC. It is one professional association among many making claims for the establishment of good practice in education. It needs, on behalf of its members, to think of how it can once again join with other groups to achieve common goals.

For twenty-five years, ASC has worked diligently to develop practice and standards that will provide a credible identity to the profession. In many institutions, the Association's aims are well on the way to being realized. Perhaps ASC can begin to believe that in a reasonable number of places there is a good enough understanding of the separate identity of student counselling for the Association to feel confident that counselling will not be diminished by allying itself with others. The subject of psychiatric cover illustrates the point well. ASC and its members know how vital it is to have access to a psychiatrist who is sympathetic to and supportive of a therapeutic approach to student problems. There are a number of physicians and psychiatrists in the British Association of Health Services in Higher Education who share that view. Yet, in contrast with the early days of student counselling, the two associations now have little formal contact. Both organizations would have a better chance of realizing their aims if they allowed themselves to make a joint case for provision. Counsellors could capitalize on the authority invested in the medical profession, and psychiatrists could use their links with the less threatening face of counselling to explain their relevance to an educational institution.

When a British prime minister can declare that there is no such thing as society, it is easy for the most rational individual or organization to operate as if no-one else cares. Student counsellors in their own institutions, and ASC as their representative organization, need to challenge in themselves the notion that they are forced to stand alone in arguing the case for student counselling. Paradoxically, they need to remind themselves that the best way to safeguard their work with individual students is to become less individual.

In the end, counselling students is, of course, what matters. Most of the time, counsellors do not know what happens to the students they see, although research and evaluation gives an anonymous view of the effectiveness of their work. Counsellors trust their judgement that the change they have perceived in their clients will last, but they can rarely be certain. Perhaps this ability to tolerate 'not knowing' is one of the reasons why counsellors sometimes find it difficult to argue as forcibly as they might that counselling is an essential part of the educational process. The evidence shows that counselling can contribute to fundamental and lasting change. Student counsellors see people who will become the husbands and wives, parents, nurses, doctors, scientists, managers, teachers and even the politicians of the future. This is reason enough to work to make sure that there is a continued and recognized place for counselling in further and higher education.

References

Acres, D. (1994a) The counsellor and new understandings of how we learn: How students can be empowered. Paper presented to the *FEDORA Conference*, Barcelona, March.

Acres, D. (1994b) *How to Pass Exams Without Anxiety*. Plymouth: How To Books.

Association for Student Counselling (1993) *Guide to Training Courses in Counselling*. Rugby: BAC.

Association for Student Counselling (1994) *Requirements and Guidelines for Members Seeking Accreditation*. Rugby: BAC.

Association for Student Counselling (1995) *Survey of Student Counselling Services in Further and Higher Education 1993/94*. ASC Research Sub-committee. Rugby: BAC.

Association for Student Counselling (undated) *Advisory Services to Institutions*. Rugby: ASC/BAC.

Bell, E., McDevitt, C., Rott, G. and Valerio, P. (eds) (1994) *Psychological Counselling in Higher Education in Europe*. Naples: La Citta de Sole.

Bell, E., Dryden, W., Noonan, E. and Thorne, B. (undated) *A Guide to Recognizing Best Practice*. Rugby: ASC/BAC.

Bond, T. (1993) *Standards and Ethics for Counselling in Action*. London: Sage.

Bramley, W. (1977) *Personal Tutoring in Higher Education*. Guildford: Society for Research into Higher Education.

British Association for Counselling (1988) *Code of Ethics and Practice for the Supervision of Counsellors*. Rugby: BAC.

British Association for Counselling (1994) *Accreditation Criteria*, Rugby: BAC.

Brown, S. (1994) in *Counselling Service Annual Report*. Hatfield: University of Hertfordshire.

Caplan, G. (1964) *Principles of Preventive Psychiatry*. New York: Basic Books.

Coren, A. (1996) Brief therapy – base metal or pure gold, *Psychodynamic Counselling*, 2(1): 28–9.

East, P. (1995) *Counselling in Medical Settings*. Buckingham: Open University Press.

Fairburn, C. and Cooper, P. (1989) Eating disorders, in K. Hawton (ed.) *Cognitive Behaviour Therapy for Psychiatric Problems*. Oxford: Oxford Medical Publications.

Fisher, S. (1994) *Stress in Academic Life*. Buckingham: Society for Research into Higher Education/Open University Press.

Funkenstein, D. (ed.) (1956) *The Student and Mental Health: An International View*. Proceedings of the First International Conference on Student Mental Health. Cambridge, MA: Riverside Press.

Garner, D. and Olmstead, M. (1983) Development and validation of a multidimensional eating disorder inventory for anorexia nervosa and bulimia, *International Journal of Eating Disorders*, 2: 15–34.

Hawton, K., Simkin, S., Fagg, J. and Hawkins, M. (1995a) Suicide in Oxford University students, 1976–1990, *British Journal of Psychiatry*, 166: 44–50.

Hawton, K., Haigh, R., Simkin, S. and Fagg, J. (1995b) Attempted suicide in Oxford University students, 1976–1990, *Psychological Medicine*, 25: 179–88.

Heyno, A. (1994) Psychodynamic counselling in practice, in E. Bell, C. McDevitt, G. Rott and P. Valerio (eds), *Psychological Counselling in Higher Education in Europe*. Naples: La Citta de Sole.

Hodgkinson, C. (1993) Peer support training, *ASC Newsletter*.

Holdsworth, R. (1994) The presidential address, in *Proceedings of the British Association of Health Services in Higher Education Conference*, Leicester, July.

Kirby, C. (1974) An organization of counsellors in a college of further education, *The Counsellor, Journal of the National Association of Educational Counsellors*, 18: 3–5.

Lago, C. (1990) *Working with Overseas Students: A Staff Development and Training Manual*. Huddersfield: British Council/Huddersfield University.

Lago, C. and Shipton, G. (1994) *On Listening and Learning*. London: Central Book Publishing Ltd.

Lucas, C. (1978) Changing concepts in student health, in *Students in Need*. Guildford: Society for Research into Higher Education.

Malan, D. (1979) *Individual Psychotherapy and the Science of Psychodynamics*. London: Butterworths.

Malleson, N. (1954) The distressed student, *Lancet*, 1: 824.

Malleson, N. (1963) *The Influence of Emotional Factors on Achievement in University Education*, Sociological Review Monograph No. 7. Keele: University of Keele.

Malleson, N. (1972a) *Student counselling: Scope and training*. Proceedings of a Conference on Student Counselling: Scope and Training. London: Department of Higher Education.

Malleson, N. (1972b) Student wastage in the United Kingdom, in E. Rudd and H.J. Butcher (eds), *Contemporary Problems in Higher Education*. New York: McGraw-Hill.

Mann, J. (1973) *Time-Limited Psychotherapy*. Cambridge, MA: Harvard University Press.

McDevitt, C. (1994) Counter-transference issues in working with students from other European cultures. Paper presented to the *FEDORA Conference*, Barcelona, March.

Milner, P. (1970) A realistic look at a Utopian fantasy, *The Counsellor, Journal of the National Association of Educational Counsellors*, 2: 10–11.
Milner, P. (1974) *Counselling in Education*. London: J.M. Dent.
Newsome, A., Thorne, B. and Wyld, K. (1973) *Student Counselling in Practice*. London: University of London Press.
Noonan, E. (1983) *Counselling Young People*. London: Methuen.
Orbach, S. (1978) *Fat is a Feminist Issue*. London: Arrow Books.
Parnell, R. (1951) Morbidity and prolonged illness among Oxford undergraduates, *Lancet*, 13: 731–3.
Payne, J. (1978) The place of psychiatry and counselling in higher education, in *Students in Need*. Guildford: Society for Research into Higher Education.
Read, J. (1974) *Warnings from the Left*. London: Pica Editions.
Richards, C. and McKisack, C. (1993) Group therapy for women with eating disorders, *Counselling*, 4(4): 270–1.
Rickinson, B. and Rutherford, D. (1995) Increasing undergraduate student retention rates, *British Journal of Guidance and Counselling*, 23(2): 161–72.
Robbins, Lord (1963) *Higher Education: Report of the Committee*. London: HMSO.
Rosenberg, M. (1965) *Society and the Adolescent Self Image*. Princeton, NJ: Princeton University Press.
Ross, P. (1993) A further look at group therapy for women with eating disorders, *Counselling*, 4(4): 272–3.
Rudd, E. (1978) The founding of the Society for Research into Higher Education, *Students in Need*. Guildford: Society for Research into Higher Education.
Russell, J., Dexter, G. and Bond, T. (1992) *Differentiation between Advice, Guidance, Befriending, Counselling Skills and Counselling*. Welwyn: National Lead Body for Advice Guidance Counselling and Psychotherapy.
Smart, P. (1970) Four years on: Some comments from the Chairman of NAEC, *The Counsellor, Journal of the National Association of Educational Counsellors*, 3: 15–16.
Swainson, M. (1977) *The Spirit of Counsel*. London: Neville Spearman.
Thorne, B. (1984) Person-centred therapy, in W. Dryden (ed.), *Individual Therapy in Britain*. London: Harper and Row.
Thorne, B. (1985) Guidance and counselling in further and higher education, *British Journal of Guidance and Counselling*, 3(1): 22–34.
Thorne, B. (1994) Brief companionship, in D. Mearns (ed.), *Developing Person-centred Counselling*. London: Sage.
Walton, H. (1978) Nicholas Malleson: Some biographical notes, in *Students in Need*. Guildford: Society for Research into Higher Education.
Wheeler, S. and Birtle, J. (1993) *A Handbook for Personal Tutors*. Buckingham: Society for Research into Higher Education/Open University Press.
Wrenn, C. (1962) The culturally encapsulated counsellor, in *Harvard Educational Review*, 32. Reprinted in *Guidance: An examination* (1965), New York: Harcourt Brace.

Index

COUNSELLING FOR YOUNG PEOPLE

Judith Mabey and Bernice Sorensen

This book gives a wide picture of the diversity of counselling services available to young people in Britain today, with special focus on schools and young people's counselling services. It sets these services in their historical context and describes how they have evolved. The book puts forward theoretical models for working with young clients and discusses counselling issues as they relate to work with this age group. In addition it considers some of the pitfalls counsellors may encounter in working alongside other professionals and within agencies. It includes discussion on ethical issues, non-discriminatory practice, confidentiality and child protection. The book is enlivened by case material and by examples of good practice and interesting initiatives from around the country. It will be of particular interest to counsellors, teachers, youth workers, social workers and counselling students interested in working with this age group.

Features
- Illustrated throughout with case material
- Wide discussion of ethical issues
- Examples of good practice and new initiatives
- Gives theoretical models for counselling young people.

Contents

The development of counselling for young people – Counselling for young people – The practice of counselling for young people – Specific issues in counselling for young people – Professional relationships in counselling for young people – A critique of counselling for young people – Appendix – References – Index.

160pp   0 335 19298 X (paperback)

COUNSELLING IN INDEPENDENT PRACTICE

Gabrielle Syme

This book demonstrates and reflects the care and responsibility that must be taken by anyone considering counselling in independent practice. It is a thoughtful book based upon the experience of a skilled and well-trained practitioner who has set her own standards high. For anyone contemplating setting up in private or independent practice as a counsellor or psychotherapist it offers an excellent model. It explores in depth the practical, ethical and personal issues that should be considered before taking such a major step. Concluding with a critique of private and independent practice, the book makes a powerful contribution to the current debate about the difference between the minimum standards set by Codes of Ethics and Practice for counsellors and what is good practice. The professional practitioner will recognize the points of discussion raised by the author. For this group, the book provides a yardstick by which to assess the quality of service they provide and the relationship that they maintain with their clients. With its useful exploration of this relationship, the book will also be of interest to anyone considering counselling or psychotherapeutic help, and those referring patients or colleagues.

Contents

160pp   0 335 19049 9 (Paperback)